Walt Disney's
Snow White
and the Seven Dwarfs
& the Making of the Classic Film

Richard Holliss and Brian Sibley

SIMON & SCHUSTER BOOKS FOR YOUNG READERS

Published by Simon & Schuster, Inc., New York

Published by SIMON & SCHUSTER BOOKS FOR YOUNG READERS,
A Division of Simon & Schuster, Inc., Simon & Schuster Building,
Rockefeller Center, 1230 Avenue of the Americas,
New York, N. Y. 10020.

SIMON & SCHUSTER BOOKS FOR YOUNG READERS is a trademark of Simon & Schuster.

SIMON & SCHUSTER and colophon are registered trademarks of
Simon & Schuster, Inc.
1 2 3 4 5 6 7 8 9 10

Library of Congress Cataloging-in-Publication Data

Holliss, Richard.
Walt Disney's Snow White and the seven dwarfs &
the making of the classic film.

Summary: Retells the Disney version of the tale
of the beautiful princess and her adventures with
the seven dwarfs she finds in the forest.
Also describes the making of the film.
[1. Snow White and the seven dwarfs (Motion picture)
2. Fairy tales.   3. Folklore--Germany] I. Sibley,
Brian. II. Title. III. Title: Snow White and the
seven dwarfs.
PZ8.H725Wal   1987   791.43'72   87-4724
ISBN: 0–671–64439–4

Produced by the Justin Knowles Publishing Group,
9 Colleton Crescent, Exeter, Devon, England

Design: Ron Pickless

Typeset by P&M Typesetting Ltd, England
Colour reproduction by Peninsular Repro, England
Printed and bound in England by
Purnell Book Production, Ltd

Dear Snow White Admirers

When I was selected to be the speaking and singing voice of Snow White in Walt Disney's "Snow White and the Seven Dwarfs" fifty years ago, little did I know that I was going to be a part of one of the greatest movies ever produced.

Indeed, it was a great honor, and it gave me great pleasure to work with Walt Disney and all the others in creating the world's first full-length animated feature. An ageless film that will continue to be seen for years to come.

Let us hope that the fine qualities of goodness and love exhibited through the character of Snow White, be an inspiration and reminder to all mankind that we can achieve happiness and great satisfaction by performing what should be the simplest task of all; that of working together with one another to achieve our personal and common goals.

With Love,

Adriana Caselotti

Adriana Caselotti

500 SO. BUENA VISTA STREET, BURBANK, CA 91521 (818) 840-1000
500 PARK AVENUE, NEW YORK, NEW YORK 10022 (212) 593-8900

8714674

THE FAIREST
ONE OF ALL

ONCE upon a time ... a Queen – a regal figure, elegant but sinister – stood before an oval mirror. Raising her arms, she uttered a curious incantation:

"Slave in the Magic Mirror –
Come from the farthest space,
Through wind and darkness I summon thee,
Speak! Let me see thy face."

A sudden, violent gust of wind caught the Queen's black robes; there was a searing flash of lightning and a deafening clap of thunder; smoke swirled within the mirror and a ghostly face appeared.

"What wouldst thou know, my Queen?"

"Magic Mirror on the wall
Who is the fairest one of all?"

"Famed is thy beauty, Majesty ...
But, hold! a lovely maid I see,
Rags cannot hide her gentle grace
Alas! She is more fair than thee."

Rage seized the Queen. "Alas for her," she cried. "Reveal her name!" The Mirror obediently replied:

"Lips red as the rose
Hair black as ebony
Skin white as snow ..."

The Queen had heard enough, she knew the name of her rival – "Snow White!"

. . .

Snow White. Fifty years on Walt Disney's animated film version of her story is as entrancing as it ever was, as fresh and magical as when it first appeared in 1937. *Snow White and the Seven Dwarfs* is also a landmark in cinema history: the first feature-length cartoon film – and the Fairest One of All.

When, in 1934, the news broke that Walt Disney was planning to make a 90-minute animated film, movie-makers and critics alike were astonished. Walt was probably the only person to whom the idea seemed not only the inevitable next stage in his personal career but also a crucial step forward for the art of animation.

But then, Walt Disney had always been an innovator. From his earliest days in the movie business he had sought ways of improving and perfecting animation techniques and was always looking for, and responding to, new challenges. In 1928, he had made the world's first synchronized sound cartoon film, *Steamboat Willie*, and launched the career of Mickey Mouse. So successful was this figment of ink and imagination that the studio was hard pressed to meet the public demand, particularly since Walt was not prepared to sacrifice quality for quantity and continued to encourage his artists to aim for greater technical excellence.

Walt also wanted to explore the full dramatic potential of the animated movie. Surely, he argued, it was possible for an animated cartoon to be both artistically pleasing and to present characters capable of expressing the same subtleties of emotion as living performers.

In 1929, Disney's desire to experiment led to a new series of short cartoons, which he called Silly Symphonies. Each was a visual tone poem in which humorous or dramatic effects were achieved by the skilful synchronization of music and movement. The first Silly Symphony, *Skeleton Dance*, featured the bony frolics of a troupe of loosely connected skeletal dancers. It was followed by such subjects as *Springtime*, *Summer*, *Autumn* and *Winter*. *The Merry Dwarfs* was one of the earliest Symphonies to use fairy-tale characters, the dwarfs of the title being grotesque little gnomes with pointed hats and beards who drank too much and then performed an inebriated dance routine.

Gradually the Silly Symphonies began to develop from musical capers to miniature dramas set to music, such as the first cartoon to be made in three-strip Technicolor, *Flowers and Trees* (1932). Disney's new departure in animated film-making was an immediate success, and with each new cartoon the Silly Symphonies became as popular with the public as the exploits of

Early forerunners of the seven dwarfs, these comic dancing gnomes appeared in the 1929 Silly Symphony, *The Merry Dwarfs*.

Mickey Mouse. They also demonstrated that the cartoon was maturing into a unique and highly effective art form.

It was during these years of technical and artistic growth that Walt began to contemplate the possibility of a feature-length animated film. After all, a cartoon feature offered practically unlimited possibilities for artistic, dramatic and technical advancement – the opportunity to tell a story that ran for longer than seven minutes, to create real characters and use them not simply to sustain a plot but to move an audience to laughter and tears.

The production of a cartoon feature was also, however, an economic necessity. Although Mickey Mouse and the Silly Symphonies had become virtually the "main attraction" on many cinema programmes, the revenue they earned bore no relation to their box-office appeal. And what money they did bring in was scarcely enough to offset the additional expense incurred by Walt's preoccupation with refining and improving his films. Production costs kept rising, substantially eroding whatever profits were being earned.

As the Depression tightened its grip on America, movie theatres were increasingly obliged to give patrons more entertainment for their money. It was the beginning of the double-feature bill, a development that left theatre managers with little running time for short subjects and not much spare cash with which to rent them.

Like Charlie Chaplin, Harold Lloyd and Buster Keaton, Disney saw that the feature-length production offered the only viable economic means of surviving difficult times.

Walt appears to have considered a number of likely film subjects. One was a film version of Washington Irving's *Rip Van Winkle*, which would combine live action and animation. However, the project had to be abandoned when Paramount, which owned the rights to the story, refused to grant the necessary permission.

Then there was *Alice in Wonderland*. As early as 1931, Walt had considered using Lewis Carroll's books as the basis of a film. He was beaten to it, however, by the Commonwealth Pictures Corporation, which, that very year, released the first sound version of Alice's adventures. Two years later, Walt was again talking about a feature-length film of *Alice in Wonderland* with Mary Pickford as a real Alice in a cartoon wonderland. Once more it was Paramount, which in 1933 thwarted Walt's plans by releasing its own star-studded version of the story.

During the same year, Walt enjoyed

phenomenal success with the Silly Symphony *Three Little Pigs*, and this further strengthened his resolve to make a feature. Discussions took place with Merian C. Cooper (the producer of *King Kong*) about the possibility of making an animated film based on Victor Herbert's operetta, *Babes in Toyland*. The project was offered to RKO, which owned the rights to the play, but was turned down.

It was also around this time that the story of Snow White was being discussed as a potential Silly Symphony. The studio had already made a number of films based on fables, folk stories and nursery rhymes – *Mother Goose Melodies*, *The Ugly Duckling* and *The Pied Piper*, for example – and in 1932, a Silly Symphony entitled *Babes in the Woods* was released. This was actually a version of the story of Hansel and Gretel, and it was a significant precursor to *Snow White* in that, in addition to the wicked witch, it featured a group of woodland dwarfs who helped to rescue the children from their imprisonment in the gingerbread house.

As one of the world's best-loved fairy-tales, *Snow White* was a likely choice for a Disney cartoon, and although the studio did not proceed with a *Snow White* Silly Symphony, Walt realized its potential in terms of animated story-telling. Much later he described it as "the perfect plot", featuring as it did a beautiful, threatened princess, an evil witch to give the story menace, a group of dwarfs for comic relief and a handsome prince to provide the romantic interest.

The tale of Snow White had first been published in Germany under the title "Sneewitchen", as part of Jacob and Wilhelm Grimm's 1812 collection of fairy-tales *Kinder-und Hausmärchen*. Eleven years later it had appeared as "Snow-drop" in *German Popular Stories*, Edgar Taylor's English translation of Grimm.

Like most of the stories collected by the brothers Grimm, *Snow White* had previously existed only as a tale handed down orally from generation to generation. But although it contains many of the classic elements of European folk tale, it is not necessarily a particularly old story, although it almost certainly contains features (such as the glass coffin) from other, older tales. Nevertheless, it is a powerful theme and one that has found its way into many different cultures around the world, including those of north and west Africa, Ireland and Asia Minor.

Many artists have illustrated the story of Snow White, and from early on it attracted film-makers. The first movie version was a 15-minute French production, *Little Snowdrop*, made in 1910. A 40-minute version of *Snow White* followed three years later, with children portraying the dwarfs. This film introduced the idea of Snow White being restored to life by a kiss from the Prince instead of following the Grimm version in which the heroine awakes when the Prince lifts her seemingly lifeless body and in so doing dislodges from her lips the piece of poisoned apple. The notion of the awakening kiss (borrowed from the fairy-tale "Sleeping Beauty") later formed a major element in the Disney version of the story.

Another *Snow White* film was released around this time by Educational Films, and in 1916 an hour-long silent movie appeared featuring, in the role of Snow White, Marguerite Clark, then a successful actress of the Mary Pickford style who had played such title roles as *The Goose Girl* and *Molly Make-Believe*.

Walt Disney poses with portraits of the characters in his first feature-length cartoon film, *Snow White and the Seven Dwarfs*.

Marguerite Clark's *Snow White* was to prove extraordinarily influential, for among the millions of youngsters who saw the movie was one Walter Elias Disney.

At the time Walt was a newsboy in Kansas City and, along with a group of his contemporaries, was invited to a screening of *Snow White*. The movie was shown simultaneously on four large screens, and from where Walt was sitting he was able to view two of them. It was, says Walt's biographer Bob Thomas, "his most vivid early memory of attending the movies".

So vivid, perhaps, that years later it encouraged him to consider the story of *Snow White* as his first full-length film – "The Feature Symphony" as he called it.

The Disney artists first learned of the project one evening early in 1934. Animator, Ken Anderson recalls that Walt gave them each 65 cents to go and have dinner at the cafe opposite the studio on Hyperion Avenue. When they returned, Walt took them to the empty sound stage, sat them down in a circle and, says Anderson, "proceeded to intrigue us from eight o'clock until early midnight acting and telling [the story of Snow White] even anticipating the songs and the kind of music, and he so thrilled us with the complete recitation of all the characters that he had created that we were just carried away . . . we had no concept that we were ever going to do anything else or ever want to do anything else. We wanted to do what he had just told us!"

Work on the film was begun by a small group of artists and writers who were given a room adjacent to Walt's office, while the rest of the studio continued to make Mickey Mouse and Silly Symphony cartoons. The first outline for the *Snow White* project, probably drafted by Walt himself, was dated August 9, 1934.

What is particularly interesting about this early record of Walt's approach to the Snow White story is that he had decided from the outset that each of the seven dwarfs should have a distinctively individual screen personality. In the version told by the brothers Grimm, and in most subsequent retellings, there was no attempt to give character to the dwarfs. One exception was the English artist John Hassall who, in 1921, illustrated an edition of the story in which the dwarfs were identified by names embroidered on their breeches. Taking his inspiration from the scene in the story where the dwarfs return to their cottage and find that someone has been sitting at their table and has taken some of their food and drink, Hassall called the dwarfs Stool,

Plate, Bread, Spoon, Fork, Knife and Wine.

In Walt's 1934 outline for the film, we find this discussion of the dwarfs, which includes five of the seven names used in the completed film:

The names which follow each suggest a type of character and the names will immediately identify the character in the minds of the audience:

Scrappy	Doleful	Crabby
Happy	Wistful	Daffy
Hoppy	Soulful	Tearful
Sleepy	Helpful	Gaspy
Weepy	Bashful	Busy
Dirty	Awful	Dizzy
Cranky	Snoopy	Snappy
Sneezy	Goopy	Hotsy
Sneezy-	Gabby	Jaunty
Wheezy	Blabby	Puffy
Hungry	Silly	Strutty
Lazy	Dippy	Biggy
Grumpy	Graceful	Biggy-
Dumpy	Neurtsy	Wiggy
Thrifty	Sappy	Biggo-Ego
Shifty	Gloomy	Chesty
Nifty	Flabby	Jumpy
Woeful		

The outline then went on to explore the potential for some of these characters and to suggest actors, for the most part radio performers, who might play the roles:

Sleepy: Sterling Holloway. Falls asleep in midst of excitement, in middle of sentence, and so forth . . .

Hoppy – Jumpy: Portrayed by Joe Twerp, the highly excitable, nervous radio comic who gets his words mixed up (flews nashes ry bichfield). He is in constant fear of being goosed but is not goosed until the last scene.

Bashful: Portrayed by Buelow, a unique radio personality with a very funny bashful laugh, halting delivery, and a way of misplacing the word "though" . . .

Happy: Portrayed by Professor Diddleton D. Wurtle, whose wild Ben Turpin eyes are reinforced by one of the funniest tricks of speech in radio . . .

Sneezy-Wheezy – Gaspy: Asthmatic inhalations and exhalations of every breath . . . Dapper . . . nimble dancer – quick movements stopped in mid-air by embryonic sneeze . . . Always trying nutty cures and diets.

The first model sheet for *Snow White* (Production No. F-1), to show animators how the seven dwarfs might be depicted.

Biggy-Wiggy – Biggo-Ego: Portrayed by Eddie Holden, in his character of Hipplewater. A pompous, oily-tongued know-it-all . . .

Awful: The most lovable and interesting of the dwarf characters. He steals and drinks and is very dirty . . .

The personalities of the seven dwarfs – or, as Walt preferred to call them, "the seven little men" – were to change and develop considerably over the next few years, and none of the suggested performers appeared on the final soundtrack, but what is quite clear is that the characters were already beginning to emerge.

The Queen, at this time was described as being "stately, beautiful in the way of a Benda mask", a cool serene character who demonstrates her fury only in moments of great passion. Various ideas for songs were also suggested, including "Some Day My Prince Will Come", which later proved to be one of the hits of the film.

The plot, as outlined at this time, closely followed the Grimm version of the story but with various fanciful embellishments, including a sequence in which, before finding the dwarfs' cottage, Snow White would journey through such enchanted places as the Morass of Monsters, Upsidedownland (where trees have their roots in the air), and Sleepy Valley with "vast poppy fields, slumbrous music from the wind soughing through the trees", which is somewhat reminiscent of the sleep-inducing poppy-field in *The Wizard of Oz*.

Some simplification took place to eliminate the traditional repetition found in the fairy-tale. For example, in the original story, the Queen – disguised as an old pedlar – makes a symbolically three-fold attempt on Snow White's life: first by lacing the child's bodice so tight she cannot breathe, second by making her a present of a poisoned comb, and finally by giving Snow White the famous apple prepared so that "whoever tasted it was sure to die".

From the outset, Walt abandoned the episode with the tightly laced bodice, but for some time the planned scenario featured both the comb and the apple. Eventually it was decided that the Queen should make only one bid to destroy Snow White and that that should be by using the poisoned apple. However, as late as March 1937 Walt suggested that a reference to the earlier attempts might be incorporated into the dialogue: "Downstairs she could be building up to the disguise – choosing something so that no one would recognize her. 'Ah, the old pedlar woman!' like she remembers it . . . 'The pedlar woman – what could she sell? – Combs soaked in poison – the hair will stiffen like a board. A corset – lace it tight!' So many people remember those old things from the fairy-tale."

And although there is no such reference in the finished film, the final page of the book shown in the closing seconds and carrying the legend " . . . and they lived happily ever after", is decorated with an illustration of a comb with strands of hair.

Walt and the studio storymen worked on the plot and characters through the autumn of 1934 at a series of meetings meticulously recorded by a stenographer. At the same time, preliminary sketches were being made by, among others, two European illustrators – Gustaf Tenggren, whose delicate water-colour designs influenced the story's rustic Germanic setting, and Albert Hurter, who created the bizarre fixtures and fittings in the dwarfs' cottage – while writer Joe Grant helped to shape the appearance and personalities of the dwarfs themselves.

Hurter joined the studio as an animator in 1932, but as Disney storyman Ted Sears recalled: "Albert's outstanding ability lay in humorous exaggeration and the humanizing of inanimate objects." He was quickly released from animation

The backgrounds for *Snow White* – such as the Queen's throne room (*above*) and the dwarfs' cottage (*left*) – were painstakingly created and contributed significantly to the film's many moods.

and set to work drawing inspirational sketches. "In a sense, he had a camera eye", wrote Sears in a posthumous sketchbook of Hurter's work, *He Drew As He Pleased*. "But the imaginative quality he put into his drawings lifted it far above the level of mere photographic accuracy."

Hurter and Tenggren not only brought to *Snow White* their own highly individual skills, they gave the film a decorative style reminiscent of the best traditions in European illustration epitomized by such artists as Arthur Rackham, Edmund Dulac and W. Heath Robinson. Early renditions of the dwarfs depicted them very much as sons of the earth: elderly, hunched and wizened figures; Snow White (contrary to the original text which describes her as having "hair black as ebony") was drawn as a blond.

There would never be another Disney feature where quite the same degree of experimentation was not only allowed, but encouraged. One story conference records that the Queen was "to be tried out as a fat, cartoon-type sort of vain-batty-self-satisfied, comedy type; and also as a high collar stately beautiful type. Sketches to be submitted and story constructed for either angle." And, indeed, trial drawings were made

During the planning stage of *Snow White and the Seven Dwarfs* Walt Disney encouraged his artists to give free rein to their imaginations. This drawing by Ugo D'Orsi shows a marked influence of such European illustrators as Arthur Rackham and William Heath Robinson.

The seven dwarfs, as they were first conceived by the Disney artists, were rather grotesque, unpleasant characters.

Early renderings of the Witch, such as this one, depicted her as a comic crone in the traditional cartoon style, which Disney himself had used in his 1932 Silly Symphony, *Babes in the Woods*.

This experimental model sheet shows early versions of the Prince, Snow White (bearing more than a little resemblance to Betty Boop) and alternative treatments for the Queen, one of which was clearly planned as a character for laughs.

"THE QUEEN" "SNOW WHITE" "PRINCE"

A sketch for a sequence later cut from the film in which Dopey accidentally swallows a spoon. Here Happy, Grumpy and Doc unsuccessfully attempt to retrieve it.

showing the Queen as a portly, stupid-looking character.

In fact the chief problem facing the Disney artists was the successful animation of the human form. Although the studio could make Mickey Mouse, Donald Duck or any member of the Disney menagerie live and breathe and accomplish impossible things, it had great difficulty in making realistic human figures achieve the simplest of movements.

To give his artists some experience of animating a pretty heroine, Walt put into production *The Goddess of Spring*, a Silly Symphony based on the story of Persephone and her abduction by Pluto, the terrible god of the underworld. Persephone had not only to move convincingly but also to "act", to convey a range of emotions from joy and happiness to sorrow and despair. She was to be the forerunner for Snow White.

Meanwhile, work on the feature continued, and at a meeting on October 9, 1934 the characters of "the seven little men" were substantially redefined:

Wheezy: Stubby – always behind or last in processions – fatter and shorter than the rest.

12

In 1934, Walt Disney made a Silly Symphony entitled *The Goddess of Spring* (*left* and *below*), which was based on the legend of Persephone. The film was an experiment in animating the human figure, and, although far from successful, it provided the animators with many valuable lessons.

Jumpy: Excitable – goosey type – talks fast – mixes up his words: as "Bee's asleep in my sled".

Baldy: Bashful – floppy ears – giggles – twists buttons – gets red in the face.

Grumpy: Stands back – deaf – sour-dough type – No teeth – glasses on – chews after speaking – lean and skinny – like Santa's secretary.

Happy: Bounces about – cut-up – Positive type – High voice – High giggle and jolly laugh – fat.

Doc: Fat – pompous and ineffectual – blustery – Nose glasses fall off at times – leader of gang.

Sleepy: Falls asleep at wrong time – fly bothers him – long lanky type untidy – one sock down.

Other names were mooted, including Hickey ("always hiccoughing at wrong moment"), Sniffy, Stuffy, Shorty, Burpy, Tubby, Dizzy (as an alternative name for Jumpy) and Dopey.

The meeting also outlined the sequence with the poisoned comb:

In one of several sequences planned for the film but not made, the Prince (*right*) was held captive in the Queen's dungeons along with (*above*) the grisly remains of similarly unfortunate young men. Finally (*opposite*), the Queen flooded the dungeon and left the Prince to drown while she went in search of Snow White.

Wild excitement as they try to revive Snow White – running for water – fanning – looking bewilderedly about – Doc's stethoscope tangles up with beard – blustery dialogue – finally he or one other points out the comb in hair – "She never had that before." Pulls it out – Snow White immediately revives – They throw comb in fireplace – greenish yellow smoke shoots up – Snow White mentions old pedlar woman – They suspect the Queen, and warn her about letting anyone in during their absence ...

On her first transformation the Queen had become a "fat, bulgy, pedlar type", next time she would take on the form of a "thin, hawk-faced, old witch type". And as she changes "warts pop out of her face – Ping! Ping! Ping!! Also, hairs out of the warts ..."

It was at this meeting and at one held a week later that Walt and his associates defined the role of the Prince. In the fairy-story itself, the Prince appears only at the climax of the tale, and although in the completed film he has very little to do other than hear and see Snow White singing at the well and then awaken her at the end, he was originally conceived as playing an integral part in the action:

Queen wants to marry Prince, but he refuses to acknowledge "that she is the fairest in the land", since he has seen Snow White ... Queen has him dragged away to think it over, or so that he will not interfere with her

diabolical plans on Snow White. Heh! Heh! Heh! is *she* a witch!

Dungeon far down below – stairs leading down – go to limit in building up creepy dark shadows – dank and dripping wet – cob-webby, musty effect – skeletons in chains – Prince gagged and heavily chained to the wall – Queen taunts the Prince – points out to him the skeleton of "Prince Oswald" chained to the wall – might have skeletons dance at Queen's bidding – Queen exits with a dirty laugh – Prince strains at bonds ...

A later refinement to his torture has the Queen begin to flood the dungeon before leaving for the dwarfs' cottage. Rescue, however, is at hand:

Birds liberate Prince – one bird steals guard's hat, and has him chase into Prince's dungeon, where Prince either socks him as he enters, or engages him in a sword duel – leaping over tables, chairs and so forth – finding his mark,

and plunging his sword into the guard while swinging on chandelier ...

Prince calls for his horse, and talks to him like Tom Mix and Tony – Horse interested in what Prince says ... seems to understand and – paws with forefoot, and so on ...

On October 22, 1934 another outline was circulated with further character developments:

Snow White: Janet Gaynor type – 14 years old.

The Prince: Doug Fairbanks type – 18 years old.

The Queen: A mixture of Lady Macbeth and the Big Bad Wolf – her beauty is sinister, mature, plenty of curves – she becomes ugly and menacing when scheming and mixing

The dwarf who proved the most
difficult to characterize was Dopey
(*left* and *below* with Doc),
although he eventually emerged as
the most lovable of the seven.

her poisons – Magic fluids transform her into
an old witch-like hag – Her dialogue and
action are over-dramatic, verging on the
ridiculous . . .

The names of the dwarfs were now listed as Doc,
Grumpy, Happy, Sneezy, Sleepy, Bashful and
"Seventh". For some time "Seventh" proved an
elusive character. "The boys couldn't seem to get
him at all," Walt later remembered. "They tried
to make him too much of an imbecile, which was
not what we had in mind. Dopey *wasn't* an
imbecile. Finally, we thought of a way to put him
across: make him human with dog mannerisms
and intellect! . . . You know the way a dog will be
so intent on sniffing a trail that he doesn't see
the rabbit right in front of him – and when the
rabbit scurries away the dog does a delayed take?
That's the way Dopey was. We made him able to
move one ear independently of the other, the
way a dog can shake off a fly. And when Dopey
had a dream, he pawed with his hand the way a

dog does while sleeping. But he had to do one
thing really well, or otherwise he'd just be stupid.
So we had him do a clever little slaphappy dance
at the dwarfs' entertainment. That let him show
off his inner personality."

The choice of the name "Dopey" was not,
however, popular with everyone. "Some of those
who worked with me, said the word was too
modern," Walt recalled. "But I showed them
that Shakespeare had used it too, so that took
care of the modernism objection. Others felt that
it would sound as if the dwarf was a hop head.
'That's not the way my mind works,' I told them.
'To me it's the best word I can think of for
somebody who's a little off-beat.'" If Shakespeare
really did use the word "dopey", the relevant
quotation has proved curiously elusive.

On November 2, 1934, a circular was issued
offering bonuses of $5 for every gag submitted for

a particular sequence and ultimately used:

> Snow White proceeds to straighten up the house. We show her picking garments off the floor, making beds, washing the dishes. The birds might help. They could bring in flowers and vases, carry out cobwebs from the ceiling or rafters. Some good gags could be used here to show Snow White and the birds busy fixing up the house for the dwarfs' return . . .

While progress was being made with the story, there was still considerable anxiety about the animators' ability to meet the challenge of drawing human figures and making them move in a naturalistic way. Walt had made every effort to train his artists and develop their appreciation of the arts. As early as 1931 he was paying for some of them to attend evening classes given by artist Don Graham at the Chouinard Art School in Los Angeles. Then the following year, Walt invited Graham to start an art training programme at the studio.

When, however, The Goddess of Spring was released in 1934, the results suggested that the problems of animating people had not yet been mastered. Considering that just a few years earlier the studio had been using the simplest black and white shapes to make crude little comic stories, the film was something of an achievement, but the heroine, Persephone, moved awkwardly and had wax-work features and rubbery arms that were more akin to Minnie Mouse than to any real girl.

Walt realized that he would not only have to improve the standard of his existing artists, but also increase the studio personnel if he was going to succeed with the Snow White project. So, in the spring of 1935, he gave Don Graham the job of recruiting no fewer than three hundred new artists. It was hard to believe that when it had made Steamboat Willie in 1928, the studio had consisted of just ten people.

Don Graham enlisted a group of diversely talented men – young arts graduates in painting, illustration and architecture – and the studio became a modern counterpart of the Renaissance master-classes. "From eight in the morning till nine at night," Graham recalled, "what was probably the most unique art school in the world was conducted. As Snow White began to take shape, various experts from all branches of the studio were called upon to contribute to the program. Intensive lectures on character construction, animation, layout, background, mechanics and direction extended studio knowledge to the youngest neophyte."

It was a lively and exciting experience for the

The sequence in which the woodland animals help Snow White to clean the dwarfs' cottage to the song "Whistle While You Work" was one of the most imaginatively animated episodes in the film. This layout drawing shows the meticulousness with which such sequences were planned.

new recruits. "We saw every ballet, we saw every film," remembers animator Marc Davis. "If a film was good we would go and see it five times. At one time Walt rented a studio up in North Hollywood and every Wednesday night we would see a selection of films – anything from Chaplin to unusual subjects. Anything that might produce growth, that might be stimulating – the cutting of scenes, the staging, how a group of scenes was put together. Everybody was studying constantly ... We weren't making much because the studio didn't have much, but it was a perfect time of many things coming together in one orbit. Walt was that lodestone."

Not that there weren't some problems arising out of this quest for artistic perfection. Animation director Ben Sharpsteen later observed that while many of the newcomers had talent and finesse "not possessed by many of the old guard artists", they were "usually sadly lacking in showmanship and entertainment". Nor did this division of skills make for easy collaboration; according to Sharpsteen it "led to many personnel problems as it divided up artists into two groups. One, that was dedicated to getting laughs – even slapstick – anything for entertainment. The other one known as the arty group ..."

And the "arty group" had a significant influence on the output of the studio, not only in terms of increased skill and competence, but also a greater awareness of the lessons that animation had to learn from other disciplines. All these things can be seen in the new sophistication of such Silly Symphonies as *Who Killed Cock Robin?*, *Music Land* and *Woodland Cafe*, as well as Mickey Mouse cartoons like *Mickey's Garden*, *Mickey's Grand Opera* and *Thru the Mirror*.

During 1935 Walt visited Europe and returned home with a wide range of children's and illustrated books, which were made available for the animators to study.

The continuity of *Snow White* was now taking shape, with each sequence of the film being discussed in the minutest detail long before any animation was begun. The following is from a meeting at which Walt, Larry Morey and Supervising Director, Dave Hand, considered the comparatively short sequence when Snow White is lost in the forest:

Larry: You will have a spider web – she runs in and turns into the web – looking back and struggles – as she breaks the vine – it swings back like a snake ...

Dave: You could have a tree, like one that

had been turned over with the roots showing, that would look like a big open mouth, and let her fall right in front of it ...

Walt: You might follow her down as she drops ... dirt and stuff can still be falling down, roots hanging out of the bank – she is hanging on one long root ... the root should break and start giving a little – then boom – let her go into the water. You start the bobbling of the logs in this shot, but don't have the alligators too obvious ...

As these sketches show, the sequence in which Snow White is lost in the forest provided the Disney artists with an opportunity to produce some dramatic story-telling.

Snow White's terrifying chase through the forest (*right* and *opposite*) is a short, but disturbing, sequence and one that established the vulnerability of the film's heroine. The anthropomorphic trees with scary eyes and branches that reach out like fingers recall the fairy-tale illustrations of Arthur Rackham, whose work had achieved great popularity in both Britain and the United States.

Walt was never at a loss for ideas, as can be seen from this extract from a story conference on October 31, 1935, at which Supervising Animator, Hamilton Luske, and staff members Harry Reeves and Charles Thorson discussed with Walt the sequence in which Snow White and the woodland creatures clean the dwarfs' cottage:

Walt: Her thought would be: "We'll get this all cleaned up before they get home and surprise them ..." We could have squirrels washing the dishes ... roll the plates along. Snow White catches squirrels sweeping stuff under the rug – corrects them. Squirrels could get plate to deer who licks it dry and shiny ...

Ham: Turn the plate and the reflection of the deer would show in the plate.

Walt: Snow White sees that – says "That's no way to do it" and puts plate back in the water ...

Ham: Find something for every animal accompanying Snow White to do, adapted to the animal ...

Harry: Raccoon would make a good duster.

Walt: Have some birds up in the rafters getting cobwebs around their tails. One gag – birds get hold of spider asleep in web – spider wakes up, wants to know what it's all about – birds throw web right into tree – spider sees where it is and says, "o.k. – it's all right with me."

Ham: Different tails could work like different kinds of mops – washing windows – one long tail would slap the water on, and another animal would squeegee the water off.

Harry: As she picks up sock, nuts fall out and squirrels make a scramble.

Ham: Dish-tub as well as table should be piled with dishes as if the dwarfs had all kinds of dishes but never got around to washing them.

Walt: Dish washing could be more or less a team work plan ...

Ham: These are such little animals that most of the work has to be done in teams – two or four to carry things.

Charles: Would a long shot of the outside of the house work well there – with dust coming out of the windows, etc.?

Snow White, shown here as a blonde, tidies-up the dwarfs' clothing – each item of which has human features and personality. This sequence was abandoned before the film went into production.

SCENE NO.	ARTIST	SCREEN FOOTAGE	B. G. DATA	DESCRIPTION OF ACTION
1	HAM	19.00		LS: S.W. enters followed by animals. dial: "LET'S SEE WHAT'S UPSTAIRS."
2	LOUIE	15.00		MCU: Animals follow S. W. - turtle starts upstairs.
3	HAM	6.11		MCU: S.W. walks up to top of stairs to landing - nods to animals - anticipating entering
4	HAM	9.09		MCU: S.W. enters through door - runs to f.g. - Dial: "OH, WHAT ADORABLE LITTLE BEDS."
5	HAM	7.11		MCU: S.W. dwarfs' bed - looks at animals. Dial: "AND LOOK THEY HAVE THEIR NAMES CARVED ON THEM."
6				CU: Four beds o.s. S.W. dial: "DOC, HAPPY, SNEEZY, DOPEY."
7	HAM	5.00		SCU: S.W. looking at dwarfs' beds. Dial: "WHAT FUNNY NAMES FOR CHILDREN.
8				CU: Three beds - o.s. S.W. dial: "GRUMPY, BASHFUL, SLEEPY."
9	HAM	24.14	SA 4C Sc 7	CU: S.W. standing by bed - yawns - Dial: "I'M A LITTLE SLEEPY MYSELF." Stretches and flops on bed - goes to sleep.
10				CU: Bird flies in - backs up in flight snaps candle out - flies off in shadow

The following appears in the header area of the draft:

PROD. NO. 2001 PROD. TITLE S.W. AND THE 7 DWARFS DRAFT NO. _____ PAGE NO. 1 DATE _____
SEQ. NO. 4 C SEQ. TITLE SNOW WHITE DISCOVERS BEDROOM
DIRECTOR 10 ASST. DIRECTOR _____ LAYOUT MAN _____ SEC'Y. _____

A page from the draft script for *Snow White and the Seven Dwarfs* giving details of the shots to be used (long shot, medium close-up, etc.) and the animators assigned to the sequence, here primarily Hamilton Luske.

Ham: Also possibility of animals who finish their jobs coming up waiting in line for something else – Snow White tells them of something else to do – or she inspects what they have done ... rubs finger over dusted furniture – finds it still dusty and her finger black.

Harry: And the animals must do it over again.

Many of the suggestions made at this meeting were incorporated into the final script, others were later abandoned, such as a whole section of the house-cleaning episode in which Snow White tidies up the dwarfs' clothing, each item of which appears to have a face of buttons, patches and stitching:

Walt: There could be character in the clothes – coats could take on form of dwarfs they belong to ... All the clothes should have sad expressions on their faces when they're in disorder and thrown about, and have smiles after proper arrangement by Snow White. One piece of wearing apparel won't smile after having the creases shaken out – Snow White pats it (or pinches its cheek) and says: "My what a grouchy look – smile, smile," and the garment changes from frown to smile.

There were to be a number of sequences planned for the film, but never used. One such scene was to have taken place on the day following Snow White's arrival at the dwarfs' cottage. After the little men were seen setting off for work, they would be shown holding what the storymen referred to as "a lodge meeting" near the diamond mine:

Doc explains purpose of the meeting.
"Listen men, we want to make a present for our little Princess, Snow White."
"Yeah, let's give her something splenderous."
"Something magnificent."
"Gorgeous."
"Beautiful, like an Angel – with wings."
Grumpy objects to the plan.
"You hollow-headed old fools – she's got you right where she wants you. Right under her thumb. All yer doin' is spoiling her. Yer lettin' her trample all over yer."
Other dwarfs object to Grumpy's attitude.

"If he don't like the Princess, then let him do what he wants to. We like her, don't we?"

"You bet we do – and the things she does for us."

"She's just like an Angel – from Heaven."

"Grumpy's an old sourpuss – ain't he?"

"Yeah – with onions."

"He don't ever like nuthin' what's nice."

Doc restores order and asks for suggestions.

"Now listen men. What are we going to give the Princess? What will it be? Something worthy of her. Something that she will like. Speak up men . . ."

"How about a pearl-handled pickaxe?"

"Or a solid gold wash pot?"

"Maybe she'd like a jewel-lined soup kettle?"

"Oh gosh, give her something nice. Like a golden harp – with Angels on it – and with wings."

Grumpy:

"Just durn fools – all of ye. A pack of nit-wits. Why don't you give her some work to do? Make her earn her board?"

The dwarfs spend a long time thinking, and then one of them comes up with the perfect solution:

Sleepy who has been quietly dozing on the forks of some tree roots, shifts his pose, stretches and yawns – saying, 'Why don't you make her a BED?'

And that is exactly what the dwarfs decide to do. From this early discussion in November 1936, the episode was expanded into a sequence

A layout sketch using not seven but nine figures to plot the action for the sequence in which the dwarfs return home after their day's work in the diamond mine.

UNIT
G

filled with whimsical comic invention. At a story conference on January 14, 1937, Walt was once again bubbling over with ideas for the scene:

Dopey is out getting material ... sees another guy – sneaks up on him and cuts off shirt tail. Dopey smiles – the guy looks around at him ... Dopey gives him a goofy smile and ... quickly cuts off the front.

We want to show the progression on the mattress ... The birds give their own feathers and the rabbits bring little tufts of their fur. The birds will make the springs for the mattress. We will show them carrying in great tendrils of vines which they will weave themselves ...

Dopey will be going around clipping off beards and bringing them back.

The beavers do the rough carving, the woodpeckers peck out the little holes while the dwarfs also carve.

Bashful is the one who is in love with Snow White. He is the sentimental one. All during the meeting he has been thinking about angels. He was the one who wanted to give

One of several episodes for the film that was planned but then abandoned was an episode in which the dwarfs build an elaborately carved bed as a gift for Snow White. Here Sneezy works on one of the bed posts (*above*) and stuffs the mattress (*right*) – a task that brings on a violent fit of sneezing.

her a harp. Then when the bed was decided upon he wanted to put angels on it. When we cut to him he is carving an angel – a cherub – on the bed and we see that a squirrel is posing as the cherub . . .

Doc is pounding out the name "Snow White" in gold. The word "Snow" is already there and he is working on the letter "W".

The bed-building was to have continued until

interrupted by the arrival of the birds and animals to warn the dwarfs that Snow White was in danger. Eventually this delightfully imaginative scene was dropped and the dwarfs were shown working at the diamond mine instead.

The studio worked hard to establish various themes to aid the film's continuity: the reappearance of the animals helped with this, as did a number of running gags such as the tortoise who was always so far behind the other animals that he arrived when everyone else was going back, or the fly which pesters Sleepy throughout the movie and which was originally going to be outwitted in the last minutes of the film when, following Snow White's awakening, Sleepy was to have trapped the insect in the glass coffin.

There wasn't a gag, line of dialogue or action that wasn't analysed, and debated: when Snow White is running through the forest, should the trees really turn into monsters or only when Snow White is looking at them? When cleaning up the dwarfs' cottage, was it was the act of a good housekeeper for Snow White to throw one of the dwarfs' pickaxes out of the window? Was it

More sketches for the bed-building sequence: the dwarfs consult their plans (*above left*), and (*left*) construct the bed using four living trees as bedposts.

Bashful's carving of an angel provides a fine example of the detailing to be found even in the preliminary sketches for *Snow White*.

Jaxon: We may not need all the prayer. The part "Have the Queen mend her wicked ways," – we want to show that Snow White doesn't hold any resentment towards the Queen.

Dick: I think she should show resentment – after all she knows that the Queen sent the Huntsman out with her to kill her . . .

Perce: I think we can get a better line than "Help the Queen to mend her wicked ways" – the line sounds pretty hokum . . .

Jaxon: One thing that we are not quite sure about is how Snow White refers to these dwarfs. What should she call them?

Perce: There might be some value to use "seven kind little men".

Dick: I would like to end the prayer on "And may my dream come true".

Dave: I'm inclined to agree with that. For instance, "Bless my seven little men of the forest – an' please make Grumpy like me", then say your line about the Queen – then "Make my dream come true" – ending the prayer with the last line about "dream".

As well as seeking to perfect the story and characterizations, Walt was striving to achieve a standard of technical excellence that surpassed the work of his contemporaries. On December 1, 1936, Walt told some of his artists: "We want to imagine it as rich as we can without splashing color all over the place. I saw Harman-Ising's cartoon about Spring . . . last night. They got colors everywhere and it looks cheap. There is nothing subtle about it at all. It's just poster-like. A lot of people think that's what a cartoon should have . I think we are trying to achieve something different here. We are not going after comic supplement coloring. We have to strive for a certain depth and realism . . . thru' the use of colors – the subduing of the colors at the right time and for the right effect . . . not try to cram everything in every sequence."

permissible for Grumpy to spit – providing he was out of doors? Or, when Snow White was to say her prayers, who and what should she pray for? An issue debated here by Wilfred Jackson, Dick Creedon, Perce Pearce and Dave Hand:

Dick: Do you think it would be cute when Snow White is saying her prayer to have a few little birds around the window who would hear her say "God bless the little birds," and get some reaction on them?

Apart from the use of colour, several other major technical difficulties had to be overcome before animation could begin on the film. Hitherto, all animation drawings had been made on sheets of paper measuring 9½ × 12in (240 × 300mm) These drawings were then traced onto sheets of celluloid the same size, painted and photographed. The animation camera could either photograph the whole drawing or select part of it for a close-up. The area to be photographed was known as the "field", the size of that field being dictated by the dimensions of the animation paper used. The maximum area of the 9½ × 12in drawing ws known as "five field", but it was soon recognized that this would not be large enough to accommodate some of the scenes planned for Snow White unless the artists were going to draw on a minute scale. The maximum area available for the artist had to be increased and a "six-and-a-half field" (12½ × 16in/318 × 406mm) was introduced – an innovation that involved designing, building and installing larger animation boards for the animators, inkers and painters and adapting the existing camera equipment.

Even these developments did not solve all the animators' problems. If, for example, the camera had to move in from a long-shot to a close-up, any figures in the distance would have to be drawn on an impossibly small scale. This was eventually resolved by devising a method of photographically reducing the animators' drawings to the required size.

Another aspect of film animation concerning Walt was its inability to give a scene any feeling of depth. When cartoons were just a series of gags perpetrated by fanciful characters, it didn't really matter whether things moved in a realistic way, but now the studio was planning to make a dramatic story with a far greater realism than had ever been attempted before.

If, in a live-action film, the camera moves into a close-up of a person, our view of anything in the foreground and background will change the closer the camera approaches its subject. In animation, a character was drawn on a flat piece of celluloid and laid over a flat, painted background so that any attempt to move in for a close-up resulted in character and background

An evocative scene from the 1937 Oscar-winning Silly Symphony, *The Old Mill*, which pioneered the use of the multiplane camera and gave a three-dimensional quality to animation.

appearing to increase in size at the same rate. The only way a more realistic effect could be achieved was to put distance between the background and the characters.

The problem was solved by William Garity, head of the studio's camera department, who developed what he called a "multiplane camera". The multiplane was a huge construction with a number of levels on which could be placed foreground details, characters and backgrounds in order to create an illusion of depth. If the camera was required to move, say, through a forest towards a figure in clearing, it became possible to remove various components of the picture to left or right as the camera got closer to give the appearance of moving *into* the scene. The multiplane was a major breakthrough in assisting the animators to create previously impossible effects.

The multiplane was used experimentally to film the 1937 Silly Symphony *The Old Mill*, which won an Academy Award. "There was nothing in it but music," Walt remarked some years later. "The story was what happened to an old mill at night; nothing more. The first scene showed the old mill at sunset. Cows wandered home. A spider wove her web. Birds nested. A storm came up and the mill went on a rampage. In the morning, when the cows wandered back, the spider's web was shattered and the birds' feathers were rumpled. The critics said, 'Poetic' but the important thing to me was the proof that I had a feeling of third dimension."

Walt's experience with making Mickey Mouse

and Silly Symphony films had taught him that sound and music were as vital to the success of a production as the visual images. However, the first attempts at scoring Snow White left him far from satisfied. It was an accepted convention of the Hollywood musical that every now and again the story would simply stop for a song or a dance. But Walt wanted to do something very different: "We should set a new pattern, a new way to use music," he argued. "Weave it into the story so somebody just doesn't burst into song."

Oklahoma!, which was first performed in 1943, is often cited as the first musical in which the numbers were an integral part of the plot; but, in fact, Walt Disney had pioneered the idea six years earlier with *Snow White*. The songs were written by Frank Churchill (who had composed the successful "Who's Afraid of the Big Bad Wolf?") and Larry Morey; and the film's background scores were by Paul J. Smith and Leigh Harline. "I'm Wishing", "With a Smile and a Song", "One Song", "Whistle While You Work", "Heigh Ho" and "Some Day My Prince Will Come" not only made a valuable contribution to advancing the story or developing characters – they all succeeded in becoming popular hits of the day.

Additionally there were several songs that were not finally used in the film. One, "The Lady in the Moon", was intended for the sequence in which the dwarfs entertain Snow White. To begin with the storymen had suggested that the dwarfs should perform a folk song such as "Little Brown Jug", "Three Blind

Pictured below and opposite are the faces behind the voices of *Snow White* as revealed in the September 1938 edition of *Film Pictorial*. Seen below, from left to right, are: Billy Gilbert, who played Sneezy; Scotty Mattraw, the stage actor who assumed the role of Bashful; Roy Atwell, who was the original Doc; Otis Harlan was Happy; Eddie Collins, discovered by Disney in a Los Angeles theatre, was to have taken the non-speaking part of Dopey; and Pinto Colvig, the voice of Goofy, was Sleepy and Grumpy. Opposite, Lucille La Verne played the Queen and the Witch; Adriana Caselotti was the voice of Snow White; while Harry Stockwell was the Prince.

Mice", "Frère Jacques", "Scotland's Burning" or "The Old Oaken Bucket", but it was eventually decided that it might be best to "make up a simple tune ourselves, and have the dwarfs sing it earnestly, working very hard to put it over – and stressing their facial and body expressions as they try to reach high or low for the notes . . ."

The song about "The Lady in the Moon" was created specifically to show the characters of the different dwarfs:

Dwarf: Once all the animals in the wood were friends, but they got into trouble . . .

Grumpy: On account of a woman!

The dwarfs would then have sung Snow White a story of how one evening all the animals fell out and fought with one another in their desire to serenade the Lady in the Moon. The dwarfs were to portray the animals in the song: frogs, crickets, mocking birds, owls and fish, which eventually discover "that she was a he and that they had been serenading the man in the moon", whereupon they forget their quarrel and become friends again. The song was later replaced by another "You're Never Too Old to be Young":

When you start to lose your figger,
And your hips keep getting bigger,
Your chest may slip but don't you fret,
No matter how weak your knees may get,
Yer never too old to be young . . .

This song was also abandoned (in favour of "The Silly Song" used in the film), although many years later it was included on some recordings, as was "Music in Your Soup", a song written for a sequence that Walt dropped from the film when it was in quite an advanced stage of production.

In the final version of the film, Snow White prepares soup for the dwarfs' supper, but before

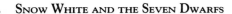

Another episode that did not make it into the completed film featured a dream sequence (*above right*) in which Snow White meets her Prince in a heavenly setting of clouds and stars. In Snow White's dream her Prince comes to her in a swan-shaped boat attended by baby stars (*above*), which blow into the sails to carry it along.

she will let them sit down at the table, she makes them go outside and wash. Only when they are all – including the reluctant Grumpy – scrubbed and clean, does she call them in to eat. The story then shifts to the Queen and her wicked scheming, and when the action returns to the dwarfs' cottage the little men are entertaining Snow White. The original script had included a comic sequence with the dwarfs eating their soup, but although it reached the stage of pencil animation, it was cut from the film continuity before it was inked and painted. Some twenty years later it was shown in this incomplete form on a Disney television programme about animation technique, "The Plausible Impossible".

The following description of the soup sequence is as Walt Disney himself described it on December 22, 1936:

There are all soup sounds, and the different ways they guzzle soup. Snow White corrects them ... "That isn't the way gentlemen would eat soup!" It is evident that she is disgusted. "Where did you learn to eat soup that way?" Doc says: "I don't know – guess it just came natural ..." She starts them out with "spoon in the hand – bend the wrist etc." and the little guys all repeat after her, and Snow White tells them that is perfect. Then they all make a terrific noise. They start in sucking the soup off the spoon six inches away from their mouths – the very thing she is trying to correct, they have not corrected.

She finally gives up in disgust ... While Dopey is eating, the suction is so terrific that he pulls the spoon right down inside of him. Until he has made a pass to dip the spoon in the soup, he doesn't discover that the spoon is missing. He looks up his sleeve and parts the soup, but doesn't realize where it has gone until he gets a "hic" and clunk ...

The rest of the sequence concerned the dwarfs' hilarious attempts to recover the spoon. During the washing scene Dopey had swallowed a cake of soap and when they finally discover a way of dislodging the spoon – with a well-planted kick on the backside – both soap and spoon emerge, the former speared to the wall by the latter. Cutting this sequence not only meant that the soap remained inside Dopey, but it also lost the impact of the change of scene, which was originally intended to cut from the bar of soap impaled by the spoon to a close-up of a heart impaled with a dagger on the clasp of the Queen's casket.

One of the film's most popular songs, "Some Day My Prince Will Come", was also intended to accompany a sequence that went through advanced stages of planning only to be abandoned. As Snow White sang to the dwarfs of the prince she hoped one day to meet, an astonishing dream sequence was to have been shown.

Walt: I was thinking, why not let her describe it up to the point where here come the stars with the Prince's ship, twinkling and carrying the ship along, pulling it with their little comet tails. They could anchor the boat to the clouds ...

Jaxon: Could some be pulling and some streaming behind with puffed cheeks, blowing the sails of the ship?

Walt: They are like a bunch of birds flying around the thing. Why not let them flap their points and get up speed?

The stars bring up the ship, the Prince gets off and comes up with a graceful bow. She does a curtsy and from that it leads into a ballet . . . a graceful little thing, and the stars turn and curtsy . . . and start dancing with each other . . .

The stars carry the train leading to the boat. All of them with their rays shooting up as the Prince and Snow White go thru'. They get on the love ship, the stars fly around it and give it a boost and as they do the wind picks it up and carries it along . . . The stars look and they are going to kiss. Maybe there's a hesitation. Then the little stars come up with bows and arrows and shoot a beam of light. It gathers around there and lights up and as the stars see it they poke their heads under the clouds . . . One little star peeks out and another pushes him in. The two are silhouetted with the cloud all light underneath them.

Intriguing though these "lost" sequences are, the story as it was finally filmed is dramatically powerful and would have gained very little from the additional scenes and songs. As it is, the plot is conveyed with great economy, and few people realize that the whole story spans not much more than some thirty hours.

With this ruthless editing, Walt had a tightly constructed story, good songs and strong characters, but, they were still characters without voices. Although there were lengthy discussions and numerous auditions, it proved far from easy to match the pictorial creations, with suitable vocal performances.

Eventually singer Harry Stockwell was cast as the Prince, and Lucille La Verne – an old hand at playing unpleasant crones in such films as *Orphans of the Storm* and *A Tale of Two Cities* – was given the dual role of Queen and Witch. Character actor Moroni Olsen was cast as the voice of the Magic Mirror, Stuart Buchanan as the Huntsman, movie actor Otis Harlan as Happy and Scotty Mattraw as Bashful. Radio actor Roy Atwell, whose routine was always peppered with hilarious muddled sentences, was signed to play Doc, while Disney studio-man Pinto Colvig doubled as Sleepy and Grumpy.

Screen comedian Billy Gilbert whose speciality was comic sneezes, read in *Variety* that

In this inspirational sketch of the dwarfs' experiment with washing, the characters are shown as having four fingers and a thumb – later simplified, to ease animation, to *three* fingers and a thumb.

One sequence that was cut from the film when it was in an advanced stage of animation featured the dwarfs eating supper cooked by Snow White and having problems with the soup.

one of the seven dwarfs was to be named Sneezy, and he immediately telephoned Walt who agreed to audition him. Once he had demonstrated his violent sneezes there was no question about who should play the part.

The hardest task was to find a voice for Snow White. Walt had his office wired up to the sound stage so that he could eavesdrop on the auditions without being swayed by the appearance of the performers. He listened to numerous young ladies but was dissatisfied with them all. One day he was confidently assured that the next singer was exactly right for the role – just 14 years old and with a beautiful soprano voice. Walt, who disliked being sold anything or anyone, listened to her and then remarked: "She's too mature; she sounds between twenty and thirty." The rejected singer turned out to be one of Hollywood's most promising young properties, Deanna Durbin, star of *One Hundred Men and a Girl.*

The search continued. Roy Scott, Disney's casting director, telephoned Guido Caselotti a well-known Los Angeles coach who was married to a prima donna from the Royal Opera House in Rome, to ask if he knew any young singers who might be suitable for the little Princess. Listening in on the telephone extension was Caselotti's 19-year-old daughter Adriana, who had some

opera training, and she promptly interrupted the conversation and began singing and talking in a young child's voice. Her father told her to get off the telephone, but Scott had heard enough and invited Adriana to the studio to audition. "They asked me how old I was," she recalls, "and although I was already 19 I said I was 17 because I realized, after they had talked to me for a couple of minutes, that they wanted someone who would be a 14-year-old-sounding girl – so I never told them my age until we were well into the film."

Adriana auditioned as had so many other hopefuls, but as soon as Walt heard her, he declared: "That's the girl! That's Snow White!"

It took 48 days to record the voice of Snow White, and Adriana Caselotti was paid $970. She had no idea, she says, quite how important the film was going to be.

One character in the story was never cast at all – Dopey. It was eventually decided that he wouldn't speak, not because he couldn't do so, but simply because he'd never tried!

Walt took as much care over allocating the characters to his artists as he did over casting voices. To animate the dwarfs he appointed Fred Moore (Mickey Mouse's animator), Bill Tytla, Fred Spencer and Frank Thomas. Art Babbitt handled the portrayal of the Queen, and Norm Ferguson the hag she changed into; Grim Natwick (veteran animator of Betty Boop) was given the seemingly impossible task of animating the Prince.

Three of the studio's younger animators – Eric Larson, Milt Kahl and Jim Algar (later a director of Disney's True Life Adventure films) – were made responsible for the creation of the little woodland creatures who befriend Snow White, and the sinister face in the Magic Mirror was the work of Wolfgang Reitherman who, for several years following Disney's death in 1966, produced all the studio's animated films.

The heroine herself was animated by Hamilton Luske. "After the picture was done," Reitherman recalled, "I remember Walt saying that Ham really held the picture together with his animation. If Snow White hadn't been believable, I don't think the rest of the picture would have worked ... even when he held her still he'd keep her dress moving to keep the animation alive. Snow White had a china-doll look to her, but in many ways, I think she's the most successful girl we ever animated at the studio."

Grim Natwick who, as well as animating the Prince, helped Ham Luske with the drawing of Snow White, recalled being allowed "two months of experimental animation before they ever asked me to animate one scene in the picture ... Disney had only one rule: whatever we did had to be better than anybody else could do it, even if you had to animate it nine times, as I once did."

In order to aid their search for realism, the animators made use of various live-action models. They studied and filmed the actions of three real dwarfs – Erny, Tom and Major George – and a baby-faced vaudeville comedian named Eddie Collins who provided much of the inspiration for the creation of the child-like

Each of the dwarfs was given a distinct personality, which was conveyed by both the drawings and the voices that brought them to life. Here six of the dwarfs turn to hush Dopey.

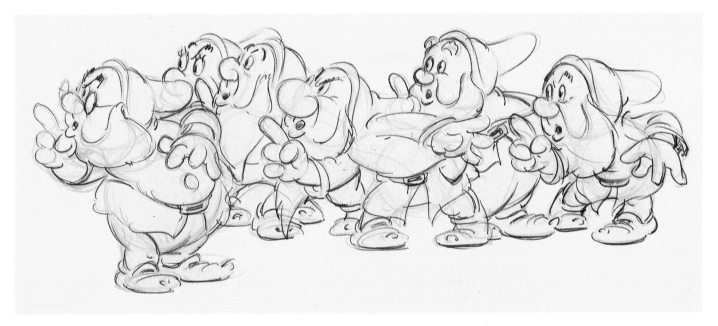

The Queen's Magic Mirror took on various forms during the planning stages of the film, as can be seen in these early sketches.

To assist the animators in the difficult task of making the characters move convincingly, articulated models were produced that could be made to assume a variety of positions.

Dopey. Louis Hightower modelled for the Prince, while Snow White's dancing and movements were enacted by Marjorie Belcher, who later found fame in the movies as half of the dance team Marge and Gower Champion.

The live-action footage that was filmed proved a valuable guide to the animators. They studied it frame by frame and based the movements of their animated characters on those of the real people. However, the process, which is known as rotoscoping, is not intended as a method of simply replicating reality. Its use, says animator Art Babbitt, is a source of reference: "Study it, study it and study it and then put it away; and then animate your impression of what you have seen, keeping in mind that the timing, the spacing and the proportions are considerably different in live action."

The use of the rotoscoping technique helped

Snow White to move realistically, but when Walt viewed some of the finished animation he was concerned that her features seemed flat and colourless. One of the girls in the ink and paint department said that she thought Snow White could use a little rouge on her cheeks and suggested that a touch of colour be added to every individual cel painting of Snow White. Walt agreed in principle but wondered how the girls would be able to place the colour accurately on each picture. They politely reminded him that they did it themselves every day.

All the component parts of the project were now coming together with one exception – money! In 1934, Walt had estimated a budget of $250,000 but when work got underway it was quickly increased to $500,000 – a figure that turned out to be approximately a third of the final cost. As expenditure on *Snow White* increased, the studio had to borrow more and more money, and there were times when Walt's brother Roy, who ran the business side of the company, was required to exercise as much commercial creativity in maintaining a cash-flow as the artistic creativity of the animators who were spending it.

Then came a day when the Bank of America baulked at advancing yet more money on a project of which they had seen nothing. Joseph Rosenberg, who was responsible for the Disney loans, had already asked the opinion of the Hollywood producer Walter Wanger who knew the Disney brothers. "Joe," said Wanger, "if Walt does as well on the feature as he has done with everything else he's made, the public will buy it." However, a great deal of money was on the line, and the cautious Rosenberg told Roy Disney that he wanted to see where the money was going. Roy told his brother: "You've got to show Joe what you've done on the picture so far."

"I can't do that," Walt replied. "All I've got is bits and pieces. You know I never like to show anybody a picture when it's all cut up. It's too dangerous."

"Walt, you'll have to," Roy insisted. "The only way we're going to get more money is to show them what they're lending money for."

Walt had no choice but to agree. The studio worked overtime preparing a presentation that would give some impression of what the completed film would look like. Parts of the story had already been fully animated in colour, but other sequences existed only in pencil animation and whole stretches of the action had to be represented with static layout sketches.

One Saturday afternoon, a nervous Walt Disney sat in the studio's projection room with

Joseph Rosenberg and showed him the first rough screening of *Snow White and the Seven Dwarfs*.

The soundtrack, like the animation, was incomplete, and Walt had to fill in lines of dialogue and snatches of song to maintain the continuity. Rosenberg sat impassively watching the screen and listening to Walt's frantic reassurances: "You remember that place back there where I had those sketches? Well, before we're through, that scene is going to be beautiful."

Rosenberg said very little apart from an occasional "yes, yes". When the screening was over he showed no indication of what he thought about the film. As Walt walked Rosenberg to his car, the banker talked about the weather and other inconsequential topics, never once mentioning the film. Walt was convinced Rosenberg's decision would be unfavourable. As

he got into his car, Rosenberg thanked Walt, said goodbye and closed the door – then, as an afterthought, he called out: "That thing is going to make you a hatful of money," and drove away.

The bankers may have been reassured, but there were plenty of others only too willing to put down Disney and his mad-cap project. Within the movie industry *Snow White and the Seven Dwarfs* was labelled "Disney's folly", and Walt was concerned that such negative publicity might adversely affect the film's chances. He sought the advice of Hal Horne, the exploitation manager of the studio's distributor, United Artists. "What should I do," asked Walt, "about all the bad talk about the feature?" "Nothing," Horne told him. "Keep them wondering. Let 'em call it 'Disney's folly' or any other damn thing, as long as they keep talking about it. That picture is going to pay off, and the more

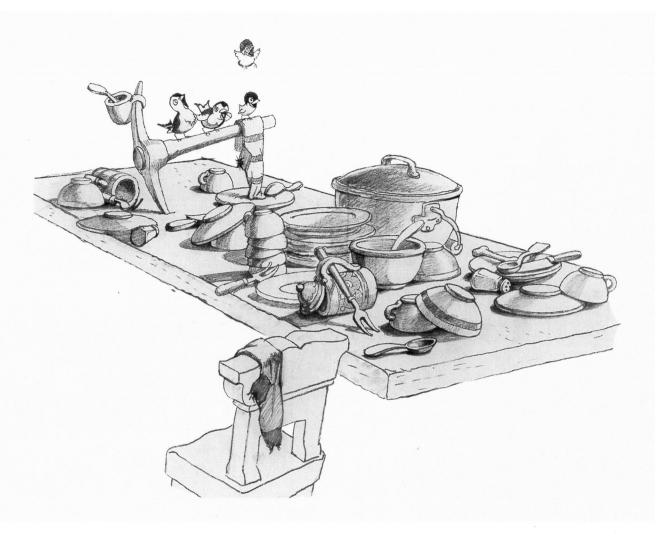

suspense you build up, the more it will pay off."

He was right, although some critics wondered whether the public would sit through a cartoon that ran for almosty ninety minutes. Writing in *Esquire* magazine in September 1937, Gilbert Seldes, a great admirer of Walt Disney, reported that he had "the exceptional pleasure of seeing ten Disney works at one time. I wanted to see . . . whether you could stand a great quantity of animated pictures without a break." Fortunately, Seldes enjoyed the experience: "I should say that you can, with excitement unabated, look at these pictures for about an hour and a half which is longer than the average feature picture. There are moments of extreme physical exhaustion if you abandon yourself to laughter, but the Disney technique is quite subtle; there are moments of suspense and moments of pure physical beauty spaced in between the great climaxes of hilarity."

Walt's chief concern by this time was to complete the movie on schedule. In February 1937, at a meeting to discuss sequence problems, Supervising Director, David Hand, had voiced anxieties that were doubtless shared by Walt: "I am awfully afraid of a weak link in this thing that is going to tie up your whole production – whether it is in the background or in the inking department or in the multiplane camera – I am afraid one department will fall down when all the rest of us have done the work."

For the next six months the staff worked against the clock. The animators came into the studio at weekends and stayed late or slept by their drawing boards on makeshift beds. There was a unique atmosphere, not just of loyalty and teamwork, but of being part of something that was about to make history. Only one dissenting voice was raised: at a preliminary screening of the partly finished film, the staff were asked for written responses, among which was an anonymous "stick to shorts!" For many years afterwards, whenever an employee made some negative response to one of Walt's ideas, he would exclaim: "I'll bet you're the guy who wrote 'Stick to shorts'!" And there are those who believe the real culprit was none other than Roy Disney.

While Walt may never have doubted the project as a whole, he was all too painfully aware of things in it that might have been done better. "I've seen so much of *Snow White*," he said at the time, "I am conscious only of the places where it could be improved. You see, we've learned such a lot since we started this thing! I wish I could yank it back and do it all over again." But by then, time and money had all but run out.

Not that Walt was prevented by that from considering remaking at least one particular sequence. Viewing the nearly completed film, Walt noticed that something was wrong with the animation of the Prince when he awakened Snow White. As he leaned down to kiss her, he shimmied. "I want to make it over," Walt told Roy who, not surprisingly, asked how much it would cost. Walt replied that it would need several thousand dollars. "Forget it," said Roy, "Let the Prince shimmy!" And so he did – and does to this day.

Eventually, at a cost of $1,488,423, *Snow White and the Seven Dwarfs* was ready for release by RKO Pictures. Previously, all Disney movies had been distributed by United Artists, but Walt and Roy had become dissatisfied with the terms, and when a new contract was drawn up that required the Disney brothers to sign away the television rights to their films, Walt decided it was time to look for a new distributor. "I don't know what television is," he argued, "and I'm not going to sign away anything I don't know about." As a result, Disney made a distribution deal with RKO.

As December 1937 approached, an enthusiastic trailer was made to publicize *Snow White*: "From Hollywood, California, motion picture capital of the world, comes exciting news! News of the completion of the most daring adventure in screen entertainment since the birth of the motion picture!"

Small wonder that *Life* magazine remarked that the film's "advance publicity has reached such proportions that Mr. Disney may well worry lest his public expect too much!"

But the studio had no intention of playing down the publicity. Referring to this "epoch-making animated motion picture", the trailer ecstatically declared the film to have been "wildly praised by public and critics alike at its premiere in Hollywood ... *Snow White and the Seven Dwarfs* is universally recognized as

something never before seen on any screen ... one of the greatest pictures ever made!" Although, in fact, that script had been written 10 days before the film had its premiere – on December 21, 1937.

Four years earlier, Walt had made *Mickey's Gala Premiere* in which caricatured stars – among them Garbo, Gable, Chaplin, Lloyd and the Barrymores – had attended the premiere of a Mickey Mouse cartoon at Grauman's Chinese Theater. Now Walt was going to have a *real* Hollywood premiere for one of his cartoons. He recalled, many years later:

All the Hollywood brass turned out for my cartoon! That was the thing. And it went way back to when I first came out here and I went to my first premiere. I'd never seen one in my life. I saw all these Hollywood celebrities comin' in and I just had a funny feeling. I just hoped that some day they'd be going in to a premiere of a cartoon. Because people would deprecate the cartoon ...

I met a guy on the train when I was comin' out. It was one of those things that kind of made you mad. I was out on the back platform – I was in my pants and coat that didn't match but I was riding first class. I was making conversation with a guy who asked me, "Goin' to California?" "Yeah, I'm goin' out there." "What business you in?" I said, "The motion-picture business." Then, all of a sudden. "Oh, is that right? Well, I know somebody in the picture business. What do you do?" I said, "I make animated cartoons." "Oh." It was like saying, "I sweep up the latrines."

Some people make you mad, and you want to prove something to them even though they mean nothing to you. I thought of that guy ... when we had the premiere of *Snow White*. And the darn thing went out and grossed eight million dollars around the world.

The premiere was a suitably glittering affair held at the Carthay Circle Theater in Los Angeles. Top executives from all the major studios were present, and among the stars who turned up in their limousines were Marlene Dietrich, Judy Garland, Charles Laughton and Elsa Lanchester.

Two people who, for some reason, were not invited to the premiere, were Snow White and her Prince, as Adriana Caselotti well remembers: "When we got to the door, the girl said, 'May I have your tickets, please?' I said, 'Tickets? We don't have any tickets – I'm Snow White and this is Prince Charming!' She said, 'I don't care who you are, you don't get in unless you've got tickets!' So, we sneaked in when she wasn't looking and we went upstairs to one side of the balcony and I stood there watching myself on the screen and all those movies stars clapping me – boy! did I get a thrill out of that!"

It was a special evening too for Walt Disney and his artists and for everyone who was about to witness the making of a piece of cinema history.

The lights went down and the curtains rose. Frank Churchill's beautiful melody "One Song" swelled through the auditorium. On the screen, the film's opening titles appeared: "A Walt Disney Feature Production – SNOW WHITE AND THE SEVEN DWARFS – Adapted from Grimm's Fairy Tales – Technicolor."

Then came a personal statement by the film's producer: "My sincere thanks to the members of my staff whose loyalty and creative endeavour made possible this production – Walt Disney"; and the list of credits, said, at the time, to be the longest in cinema history. Next, a huge gold-embossed, leather-bound book was seen, opened by invisible hands to a page of illuminated text . . .

Once upon a time …

there lived a lovely little Princess named Snow White. Her vain and wicked Stepmother the Queen feared that some day Snow White's beauty would surpass her own. So she dressed the little Princess in rags and forced her to work as a scullery maid.

Each day the Queen consulted her Magic Mirror:
"Magic Mirror on the wall, who is the fairest one of all?"
And as long as the Mirror answered "You are the fairest
one of all", Snow White was safe from the Queen's
jealousy. But one day the Mirror gave a very different answer.

"Magic Mirror on the wall —
Who is the fairest one of all?"

"… A lovely maid I see —
Rags cannot hide her gentle
grace —
Alas, she is more fair than
thee."

Unaware of the Queen's anger, Snow White worked
away, singing to the doves that came to watch. That day
a Prince came to the castle. Captivated by Snow
White's beauty, he fell in love with her.

"I'm wishing . . . for the one I
love to find me today."

"Now that I've found you
Hear what I have to say.
One song, I have but one song –
One song only for you.
One heart tenderly beating,
Ever entreating, constant and
    true."

But Snow White and the Prince did not know that the jealous Queen was planning Snow White's death.

"Take her far into the forest. Find some secluded glade where she can pick wild flowers . . . and there, my faithful Huntsman, you will kill her. But to make doubly sure you do not fail, bring back her heart. . ."

The Huntsman watched Snow White as she picked
flowers and talked to a baby bird. Quietly, he took out
his knife and crept towards her.

"What's the matter? Where's
your mama and papa? Why, I
believe you're lost. Oh, please
don't cry."

The Huntsman was poised to strike, but suddenly he fell
to his knees, urging Snow White to flee for her life.
She ran in terror through the dark wood, branches
catching at her dress.

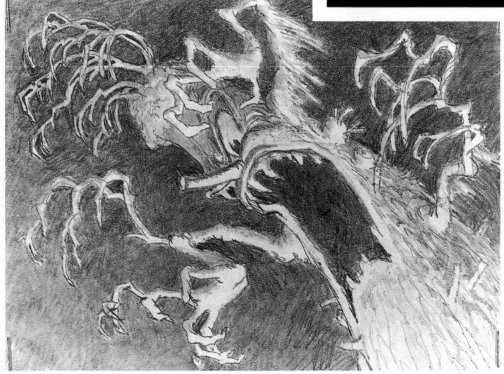

"I can't do it – forgive me – I
beg of your Highness, forgive
me. . . . Now quick, child. . . .
Run, run away – hide. In the
woods, anywhere, never come
back. . . . Run – run – hide."

She collapsed on the ground exhausted. When she awoke, she was surrounded by friendly animals.

"Please don't run away . . . I won't hurt you. Everything's going to be all right . . . but I do need a place to sleep at night. . . . Maybe you know where I can stay."

The animals led her deep into the woods until, in the middle of a forest glade, they came across a tiny cottage.

"Oh, it's adorable. Just like a doll's house."

No one seemed to be at home, so the animals followed
her inside.

"Oooh – it's dark inside."

"What a pile of dirty dishes . . .
And just look at that broom!"

There were cobwebs everywhere, but Snow White and
the animals soon had everything spotless.

"Why, they've never swept this
room."

"I know, we'll clean the house
and surprise them . . . then
maybe they'll let me stay."

"Just whistle while you work
 And cheerfully together we can
  tidy up the place.
 So hum a merry tune –
 It won't take long when there's
  a song
 To help you set the pace. . . .
 So whistle while you work.
 When hearts are high
 The time will fly
 So whistle while you work."

Upstairs Snow White and the animals found seven little beds.

"Oh, what adorable little beds. And look – they have their names carved on them. Doc – Happy – Sneezy – Dopey. What funny names for children. . . . Grumpy – Bashful – and Sleepy."

"I'm a little sleepy myself."

Not far away, the real owners of the cottage, the Seven Dwarfs, were hard at work in their mine, digging for diamonds, rubies and other precious stones.

"We dig – dig – dig – dig – dig –
    dig – dig
In our mine the whole day
    through.
To dig – dig – dig – dig – dig –
    dig – dig
Is what we like to do."

"We dig up diamonds by the
    score
A hundred rubies – sometimes
    more –
Though we don't know what
    we dig 'em for
We dig – dig – dig-a-dig – dig!"

Having finished their work for the day, they all followed
Grumpy out of the mine, singing as they went.

"It ain't no trick
 To get rich quick
 If ya' dig- dig- dig-
 With a shovel or a pick.
 In a mine –
 In a mine —
 In a mine –
 In a mine —
 Where a million diamonds
 Shine."

"Hi-ho, hi-ho
 It's home from work we go."

The dwarfs sang all the way home. They were looking forward to their supper when they saw a light in their cottage.

"Look our house – the lit's light – the light's lit! Door's open – chimney's smokin' – Somethin's in there."

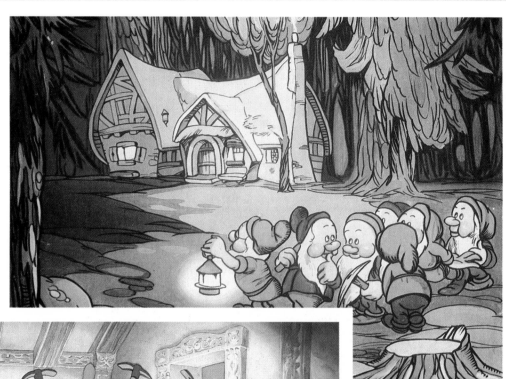

"Careful men, search every crook'n nanny – uh, hook'n granny – uh, crooked fan – uh, search everywhere."

"Don't be afraid – we're right behind you."

The dwarfs tiptoed into their bedroom.

"Gee what a monster! Covers three beds! Let's kill it 'fore it wakes up."

"Why – i-i-i-it's a girl."

"Now don't tell me who you are – let me guess. . . . If you let me stay – I'll keep house for you – I'll wash –and sew – and sweep – and cook . . . plum pudding and gooseberry pie."

The dwarfs were delighted that Snow White was going
to cook supper for them, but she insisted that they wash
first. Doc explained what they had to do.

"Supper's not quite ready.
You'll just have time to wash."

"Come on, now, men. . . .
No – now don't get excited –
here we go. Step up to the tub
– tain't no disgrace. Just pull up
your sleeves and get 'em in
place. Then scoop up the
water, and rub it on your face,
and go brrr – brrr – brrr."

In her castle the Queen went to the Magic Mirror,
gloating that she held Snow White's heart in the casket.
But the Mirror told her that Snow White still lived, and
in fury the Queen descended to the castle dungeon
where she mixed a strange magic potion.

"Over the seven jeweled hills –
Beyond the seventh fall,
In the cottage of the seven dwarfs
Dwells Snow White,
Fairest one of all. . . .
Snow White still lives
The fairest in the land.
'Tis the heart of a pig
You hold in your hand."

"I'll go myself . . . to the dwarfs' cottage in a disguise so
complete . . . no one will ever suspect."

At the cottage, Snow White and the Seven Dwarfs,
unaware of the Queen's evil schemes, were
having a party.

"... I like to dance
And tap my feet, but they
won't keep in rhythm.
You see, I washed 'em both
today and I can't do
nothin' with 'em."

Snow White sang to the dwarfs about her dream Prince.

"Some day my Prince will
   come,
Some day we'll meet again,
And away to his castle we'll go
To be happy forever, I know."

"Some day when spring is here
We'll find our love anew,
And the birds will sing
And wedding bells will ring.
Some day when my dreams
   come true."

"Bless the seven little men who
have been so kind to me – and
– and may my dreams come
true. Amen."

Now transformed into an ugly pedlar woman, the
Queen read aloud from her book of spells.

"And now . . . a special sort of death for one so fair. What shall it be?"

"A poison apple! Sleeping death. One taste of the poisoned apple, and the victim's eyes will close forever . . . in the sleeping death."

"When she breaks the tender peel to taste the apple in my hand, her breath will still, her blood congeal. Then I'll be fairest in the land."

"The victim of the sleeping death can be revived only by love's first kiss. No fear of that. The dwarfs will think she's dead. She'll be buried alive."

The next morning Snow White saw the dwarfs off to work. As she was busy making a gooseberry pie for their supper, she was startled by the croaking voice of an old pedlar woman.

"Now, I'm warning ya' . . . Don't let nobody or nothin' in the house."

"All alone my pet?"

"It's apple pies that make the men folk's mouths water."

The Witch offered the poisoned apple to Snow White who bit into it.

"I'll share a secret with you . . . This is no ordinary apple. It's a magic wishing apple . . . one bite and all your dreams will come true. . . . There must be something your little heart desires. . . . Now take the apple, dearie – and make a wish."

"Now I'll be fairest in the land."

The animals and birds had sensed that there was
something evil about the old pedlar woman, and they
rushed to the mine to warn the dwarfs.

"The pesky critters won't
stop.... There's somethin'
wrong.... They ain't actin'
this way for nothin'.... Maybe
the old Queen's got Snow
White.... We've got to save
her."

"There she goes . . . after her."

As a fierce thunderstorm raged around her, the Witch screamed at the dwarfs.

"I'm trapped! What will I do? The meddling little fools."

"I'll fix you! I'll fix you! I'll crush your bones."

Suddenly, a lightning bolt struck the cliff edge, and the stunned Witch fell backwards, never to be seen again.

. . . So beautiful, even in death, that the dwarfs could not find it in their hearts to bury her. . . . They fashioned a coffin of glass and gold, and kept eternal vigil at her side. . . . The Prince, who had searched far and wide, heard of the maiden who slept in the glass coffin.

"One song, my heart keeps singing
One song – only for you."

The Prince awakened Snow White with a kiss.

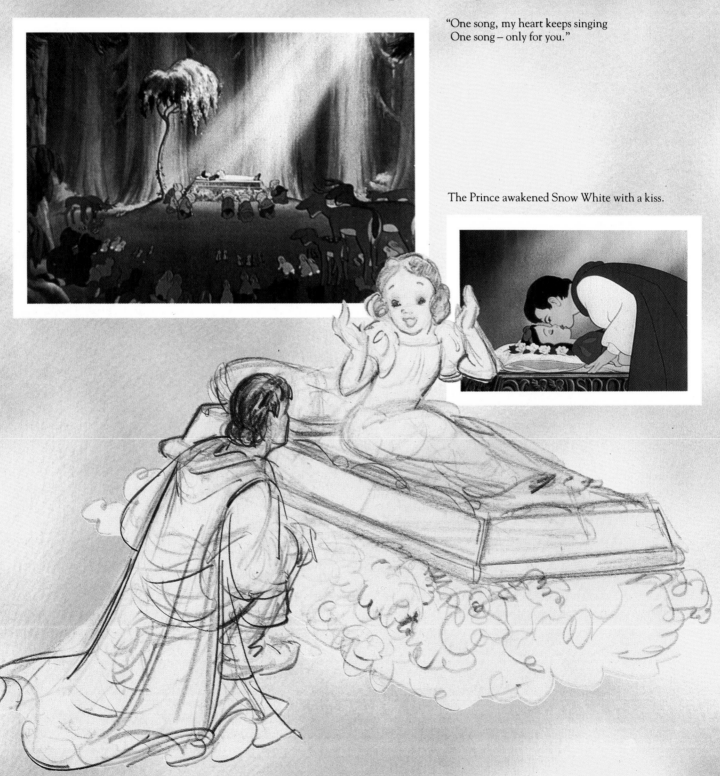

The dwarfs danced for joy as the Prince lifted Snow
White onto his horse. She said goodbye to the dwarfs,
and they rode off to the Prince's castle. . .

... and they lived
happily ever after.

As the house lights came up, the audience – already applauding – rose to its feet, hardened movie moguls and their wives wiping their tear-moistened eyes. For what, only 83 minutes earlier, had been known by all of Hollywood as "Disney's folly", was now part of cinema legend.

"It was the most receptive, enthusiastic audience I have ever seen," recalled Disney animator Shamus Culhane. "Every song, every gag, every good piece of acting worked on those people like a bow on a fiddle. There was almost continuous laughter and applause until Frank Thomas' sequence, where the sorrowing dwarfs gather around Snow White's bier. The house fell silent, gripped by the emotional impact of the acting. It was the first time grief had been so dramatically depicted in an animated cartoon."

The critics were equally ecstatic. Howard Barnes wrote in the *New York Herald Tribune*: "After seeing *Snow White and the Seven Dwarfs* for the third time, I am more certain than ever that it belongs with the few great masterpieces of the screen. It is one of those rare works of inspired artistry that weaves an irresistible spell around the beholder.... *Snow White and the Seven Dwarfs* is more than a completely satisfying entertainment, more than a perfect moving picture, in the full sense of that term. If offers one a memorable and deeply enriching experience."

Time claimed that the film was "as exciting as a western, as funny as a haywire comedy, as sad as a symphony", while in the *New York Times*, Frank S. Nugent wrote: "Mr. Disney and his amazing technical crew have outdone themselves. The picture more than matches expectations. It is a classic, as important cinematically as *The Birth of a Nation* or the birth of Mickey Mouse."

In England the reviewer for the British Film Institute said that "to see the film is to see into Fairyland", while Basil Wright commented in *The Spectator*: "*Snow White* engrosses the attention from beginning to end. So convincing is it that it is difficult at times to realize that one is watching the painted figments of an animation table with no life beyond their creator's pencils and brushes."

Of course the film had its critics – animator Max Fleischer, creator of Popeye, thought it "too arty" – but even the critics were hard pressed to find much wrong, most criticism being levelled at the stiffness and awkwardness of the human characters compared with the fluidity of the dwarfs and forest animals.

Punch objected to the film's "human" stars: "Grimm has been rather roughly handled and Americanized," wrote the magazine's reviewer, E. V. Lucas. "Snow White herself, whom we have always thought of as a charming little girl, wavers between the naïvest simplicity and adult sophistication, and speaks in a voice in which the accents of Betty Boop are far too prominent; the Prince is sheer pasteboard; the hard-boiled dwarfs are a shade too realistic, and the Queen, as the jealous stepmother, is of malignity compact, and, as the witch, an unholy terror." This irritated journalist even thought the film was too long – "Disney films must not be full length," he demanded – but even Lucas admitted to liking Snow White's animal friends.

Frank Nugent, writing in the *New York Times*, agreed wholeheartedly. "The little bluebird who overreaches itself and hits a flat note to the horror of its parents; the way the animals help Snow White clean house, with the squirrels using their tails as dusters, the swallows scalloping pies with their feet, the fawns licking the plates clean, the chipmunks twirling cobwebs about their tails and pulling free; or the ticklish tortoise when the rabbits use his ribbed underside as a scrubbing board – all these are beyond a youngster's imagination, but not beyond his delight."

Certain elements of the story were considered by some critics to be a little frightening for children. When challenged on this subject, Walt Disney told parents: "I showed *Snow White* to my own two daughters when they were small, and when they came to me later and said they wanted to play witch, I figured it was all right to let the other kids see the film." Even though Diane, one of Walt's daughters, confessed that she hid her face in her hands when the witch appeared on the screen, it was just a completely natural reaction that all children experience. As long as a film ends happily, most children quite enjoy being frightened, and, like all Disney films, *Snow White and the Seven Dwarfs* underlined the triumph of good over evil. Besides, the film was no more frightening than the original story – in some respects, in fact, less so.

Whatever the comments, the film went on to

Time Magazine honoured Walt Disney with a cover on December 27, 1937, one week after the world premiere of *Snow White and the Seven Dwarfs*.

become a financial block-buster. It ran for an amazing five weeks at the New York Radio City Music Hall, and was removed only because Walt and Roy were concerned that its impact on regional cinemas might be dissipated if it was held over any longer.

Letters from an appreciative public poured into the studio. One man wrote: "Before seeing *Snow White* I was 53 years old, now I'm 53 years young. . . . You have carried me back to the happiness and safety of my childhood." Another wrote to say: "There's a motto which I have tried to carry out as much as possible in my living – it's this: 'Be the best.' With *Snow White* I believe you have achieved the most delicate iota of every nuance that may be conceivably inferred from that motto."

Such was the critical attention given to *Snow White* that intellectuals sat up and took notice, and began to discover animation as an art form. Among the eminent writers who discussed the film's artistic qualities was art critic Jean Charlot, who wrote in 1939: "Disney's creations are no vagaries. They are shapes modelled strictly along the lines of their function and their function burgeons into beauty. When Doc turns around and the sphere of his skull melts blushingly into the twin sphere of his nose, one gets an impact of functional beauty. For Doc is fully consistent with the cinema as Raphael's Virgin is consistent with paint."

Cinema-goers who were interested in art must have been thrilled when, in August 1938, the *Hartford Times* of Connecticut reported: "The Walt Disney Studios have signed a contract with the Courvoisier Art Gallery of San Francisco for the worldwide distribution of original work not only from *Snow White and the Seven Dwarfs* but from future Disney productions and short subjects as well."

Approximately 7,000 celluloid paintings were selected for sale, the others being destroyed. The studio claimed the pressure to sell off its artwork came not only from the public, but also from museums and art collectors. Each cel bore the following declaration: "This is an original painting on celluloid from the Walt Disney Studios, actually used in the filming of *Snow White and the Seven Dwarfs*. Only a very limited number have been selected to be placed on the market. Walt Disney."

The *Philadelphia Record* noted with interest in October 1938: "They took down the immortal picture of Whistler's Mother from its time honored spot on the walls of the Charles Sessler Galleries . . . yesterday, and in its place they hung a portrait of – Dopey! Down came the

Rembrandts, the Dürers and the works of the old masters. And up went the pictures of Grumpy being doused in the watering trough, a scene showing Sneezy and Dopey dancing with Snow White, the turtle rolling down the steps and other now famous scenes from . . . *Snow White and the Seven Dwarfs*." The article went on to point out that, among collectors, Happy was the most popular dwarf, with Dopey running a close second. The sale of this artwork brought in a profit of over $15,000 to the studio.

Over forty years later, in an auction at the Sotheby Parke Bernet Gallery, Los Angeles, in May 1982, a celluloid of Snow White and some forest animals, signed by Walt Disney, sold for $425, while a scene of Dopey and Sleepy, also signed, fetched $575. In November 1986, an auction at Christie's, New York, featured a celluloid and background of the Witch at her cauldron – it was sold for $30,800.

The demand for foreign versions of the film was so great that it was dubbed into 10 languages, with the dwarfs acquiring some interesting new names: Doc became Prof in French; Grumpy, Sleepy and Dopey were rechristened Butter, Trotter and Toker in Swedish; while Happy became known as Gongolo in Italian, Bashful as Romántico in Spanish and Sneezy as Apsik in Polish.

Always a perfectionist, Walt insisted that foreign-language versions of the film had specially prepared backgrounds to suit the individual country. In Italy, therefore, the storybook seen at the film's opening, the calligraphic writing in the witch's book of spells and even the carved names of the dwarfs on the ends of their beds were repainted on the backgrounds in Italian. This attention to detail was unheard of and extremely costly. But Disney knew that *Snow White* was worth it.

And worth it the film most certainly was. By the outbreak of World War II, *Snow White* had grossed over $8 million worldwide. This was a phenomenal sum, particularly since the film was being seen by a great number of children, which meant reduced ticket rates. Only in Great Britain was the box-office take slightly deceiving. It had been decided in some parts of the country that *Snow White* should carry an "A" certificate and be advertised as usuitable for small children. This partial ban was lifted only when the film was re-issued in the mid-1950s.

Walt decided to put the earnings from *Snow White* to good use, and in August 1938 he and Roy put a deposit of $10,000 on a 51-acre site in Burbank, California. The total purchase price of the property was $100,000, and the studio

FIFTEEN CENTS   December 27, 1937

TIME

The Weekly Newsmagazine

Color photograph for TIME by Robert Mack

**HAPPY, GRUMPY, BASHFUL, SNEEZY,
SLEEPY, DOC, DOPEY, DISNEY**
The boss is no more a cartoonist than Whistler.
(See CINEMA)

Volume XXX   Number 26

Circulation Office, 330 East 22nd Street, Chicago.   (Reg. U. S. Pat. Off.)   Editorial and Advertising Offices, 135 East 42nd Street, New York.

A German poster used for a
mid-1970s re-issue of *Snow White
and the Seven Dwarfs*.

Opposite: A poster for the first
French release of *Snow White* in
1938, which was drawn by B. Lancy
in a highly individual style, very
different from that of the movie.

complex that Walt was planning to build cost
$3.8 million. It was a huge outlay, but his
confidence in the continuing box-office success
of *Snow White* and his plans for topping that
success with his second animated feature,
Pinocchio, persuaded him that it was worth the
financial gamble.

Compared with the old Hyperion Studio, the
new facilities were luxurious. Apart from an
enormous animation building, there were a
sophisticated sound stage, cutting-rooms, sound
departments and new offices, all carefully
landscaped to be conducive to a good working
atmosphere. When Walt's father, Elias,
wondered what use the studio would have if it

failed to work as an animation business, Walt put
his mind at rest by conveniently creating the
myth that it could easily be transformed into a
hospital. Although that never proved necessary,
the studio was used by the armed forces during
World War II. And it was from that unlikely
background that Walt found new employment
for some of Snow White's friends.

In 1941 John Grierson, the British
documentary film-maker and Commissioner of
the National Film Board of Canada, signed a
deal with Disney to produce some public service
films explaining the importance of purchasing
Canadian war bonds. The first featured the
Three Little Pigs, the second, starring Doc,

Grumpy, Happy and the rest, was entitled *7 Wise Dwarfs*. The film opened with stock footage of the mine sequence, followed by the original animation of the dwarfs to new backgrounds, as, to the tune of "Heigh Ho", they marched off to the bank with their sacks of diamonds to buy Canadian war bonds. The dwarfs, together with Snow White, Bambi and Figaro (from *Pinocchio*) were used also to decorate a special certificate presented by the United States Treasury to purchasers of war bonds.

Such was the success of *7 Wise Dwarfs* that the U.S. Office of the Coordinator of Inter-American Affairs commissioned a series of educational films for South America. One of these, *The Winged Scourge*, featured the dwarfs. Released in January 1943, the film showed how the seven dwarfs combated the risks of malaria by clearing mosquito breeding grounds with a variety of sprays and cleaning techniques. At the end of the film the dwarfs were seen sleeping under the security of their mosquito nets. The

Above and *right:* The dwarfs protect their home against invasion by the malaria-carrying anopheles mosquito in *The Winged Scourge* (1943), an educational film commissioned by Nelson Rockefeller for the U.S. Office of the Coordinator of Inter-American Affairs.

British government was so impressed with the film that it bought some prints for use in India. Unlike *7 Wise Dwarfs*, *The Winged Scourge* used all new animation, but it was the last time the dwarfs appeared in a Disney film.

Before the war was over, however, they had appeared on numerous insignia, specially designed by the studio for the armed forces. The dwarfs were somewhat incongruously shown building aircraft, mine-sweeping or even occasionally dropping bombs – although always, it must be said, with a disarming smile.

The distributors cried out for more dwarfs just as they had requested more pigs after the hugely successful *Three Little Pigs*, but although Walt had allowed his colleagues to persuade him to make sequels to *Three Little Pigs*, none of them were box-office hits, and he had no intention of repeating the mistake with *Snow White*.

At the Academy Award ceremony on February 23, 1939, Walt Disney received a special Oscar for *Snow White*. Consisting of one

During World War II the Disney studio received hundreds of requests from different units of the American armed forces (and some from overseas) for specially designed insignia. Shown here are some of the results featuring Snow White and the dwarfs. Making an appearance as Doc's patient (*left*) is Thumper from Walt Disney's 1942 film, *Bambi*.

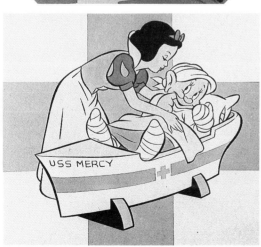

In 1939, the Academy of Motion Picture Arts and Sciences presented a special Oscar (and seven miniatures) to Walt Disney for *Snow White and the Seven Dwarfs*. The presentation was made, standing on a chair, by nine-year old Shirley Temple. Walt announced that he was so proud of the award he was going to burst, and the child-star brought the house down by exclaiming, "Oh, don't do that, Mr Disney!"

large statue and seven small Oscars mounted on a plinth, the inscription read: "To Walt Disney for *Snow White and the Seven Dwarfs* recognized as a significant screen innovation which has charmed millions and pioneered a great new entertainment field for the motion picture cartoon." The award was presented by nine-year-old Shirley Temple. "Isn't it bright and shiny?" she asked. "Yes," Walt replied. "I'm so proud of it."

In July 1940 *Snow White* was issued in America and Canada together with four shorts under the title *The Walt Disney Festival*, partly to offset the poor box-office takings of *Pinocchio*, which had been released in February 1940. When *Snow White* was re-issued in 1944 it was accompanied by a massive publicity campaign, with a lot of attention being focused on Dopey. "Requests for pictures of Dopey and the other characters poured in by the hundreds," reported the film's campaign book for that year. "The letters expressed all shades of appreciation from simple enjoyment of the picture to amazement at its reality and to enthusiastic praise of technical excellence. One woman wrote: 'Criticizing *Snow White* is like telling Titian to correct his colors.'"

To help publicize the film, Walt asked Adriana Caselotti, the voice of Snow White, to make a promotional tour of America accompanied by Pinto Colvig, the voices of Sleepy, Grumpy and Mickey's pal Goofy, and Clarence Nash, the voice of Donald Duck. Having had to accept anonymity until that time, she jumped at the opportunity. "Walt felt that each person was only contributing a small part of the picture, that the singers were not as important as the animators," Adriana recalls. "I'm not complaining though, as there were a lot of compensations – I toured all America as Snow White and they paid me $300 a week, which was a lot of money in those days, especially for a kid."

Adriana was even called upon to promote subsequent Disney movies, including 1946's *Song of the South*. On each tour Adriana dressed in a costume identical to the one worn by the film's heroine. "On one occasion," she says, "I lost all my luggage, except for my Snow White costume, and for two weeks I had to travel around in this silly dress. I felt very foolish. I was 35 years old, and I overheard one little girl say to another, 'Oh, isn't she old'." Perhaps her experiences contributed to her decision not to undertake any tours when the film was re-issued in 1952.

Although Adriana's voice was far too distinctive ever to be used in another Disney movie, she became perhaps the most famous and recognized cartoon voice of all. In 1961 a Snow White Grotto was built beside the Sleeping

Beauty Castle in Disneyland. The Grotto featured exquisitely carved figures of Snow White, the dwarfs and some of the animals, but the sculptors lacked the animators' discipline of scale and carved Snow White the same size as the dwarfs. By cunningly arranging them with Snow White a little way above the dwarfs, a convincing false perspective was achieved.

Beside the Grotto stands a Wishing Well, where passers-by can make a wish and drop in a coin or two to help the work of children's charities throughout the world. Every few minutes the Snow White figure in the Grotto sings the famous song "I'm Wishing", and the Well sings back the echo. Until 1983 the singing had been taken from the original film soundtrack, but, with the opening of the park's new Fantasyland, it was decided to invite Snow White's real voice back to re-record the song. "It was quite a challenge," Adriana remembers. "I was already 67 years old, and didn't know if I could sound exactly the same as I did in 1937. They had already recorded the orchestra, so I had to sing in the same key as I had in the film." Despite her anxiety the recording went perfectly, although Adriana admitted to quietly asking for Walt's assistance with the humming. "Walt," she whispered, "If you're anywhere along here, I need your help." Snow White and her echo sang once more.

Adriana, who lives in a Hollywood cottage with a wishing well in the garden, looks back on the film with a great deal of affection. "It was the most wonderful experience of my life. I helped create a little bit of magic. I haven't yet come down to Earth. Snow White became part of my life and has been with me ever since."

Perhaps it is because the film is so much a part of everybody's life that some of the catchphrases used to promote the movie seem to have made such heavy weather of a relatively simple task. In the early 1950s, for instance, it was described as: "The show thrill of your life time . . . thrill to its magic beauty . . . its glorious tunes . . . the comic pranks of the lovable dwarfs . . . all its excitement and enchantment. . . . The one and only Disney's great picture . . . aglow with miracle beauty . . . gay with the pranks of Dopey and his happy little pals. . . . RKO Radio releases what myriads of enchanted beholders have termed the greatest picture of all time."

The film was re-released in America in 1952, 1958 and 1967, on the last occasion as a tribute to Walt Disney who had died the previous December. It was reissued again in 1975, 1983 and 1987.

Writing in *Movies for Kids* in 1973, Ruth Goldstein and Edith Zornow warmly recommended *Snow White*: "There are few movies whose faults don't matter, because you're too busy enjoying their radiance to notice. *Snow White* is pure gold for children, for any number of reasons – seven to begin and end with, for the dwarfs are inspired creations: half a dozen more if you remember songs like 'Just Whistle While You Work' and 'Heigh Ho'."

And gold was an appropriate word to use to describe a film that generated an astonishing merchandising bonanza. Mickey Mouse and, to some extent, the Three Little Pigs, Donald Duck, Pluto and Goofy, had already been successfully merchandised for a number of years, bringing a useful revenue to the studio as well as helping manufacturers to sell their products. Everyone was quick to see the potential offered by Snow White and her seven little men.

A special foyer display advertising *Snow White and the Seven Dwarfs* on its first release in 1938. The characters, who were still to become established, carry names for easy identification.

Likenesses of the characters were soon adorning babies' rattles, nursery tea-sets, lampshades, bed-spreads and carpets, lunch-tins, sandwich trays, fork and knife sets, and cake frills. There were Snow White slippers, toothbrushes and hairbrushes, oilskin raincapes for little girls and Dopey umbrellas. Paris Neckwear of New York produced a range of Snow White ties, each featuring one of the dwarfs, while women could buy expensive items of Snow White jewellery. Children could save up to buy a Snow White piano or a set of marionettes by keeping their money in a Dopey coin bank, and they could celebrate a birthday with a fancy-dress party wearing Snow White masks and costumes and playing any one of a number of Snow White games or they could cut out various scenes from the film printed

Playing cards from the *Snow White and the Seven Dwarfs* card game, produced in Britain by Pepys and described as "The 'Prince' of Card Games" and "The Game for 'Happy' Hours".

A three-dimensional greetings card from "Snow White and her Forest Friends" and featuring a scene from the film; the card was printed in Britain during the late 1930s.

One of the many sets of figurines modelled on the *Snow White* characters.

Walt Disney (*below*) in thoughtful mood, contemplates the seven little men whose antics helped make *Snow White and the Seven Dwarfs* an international success.

on the back of Post Toasties cereal packets.

A Snow White radio appeared on the market in 1938, and Ingersoll produced an attractive watch depicting Snow White lifting her skirts in a curtsy and marketed in a box containing a reproduction of an original movie cel.

Richard G. Krueger Inc. of New York manufactured Snow White and the dwarfs character dolls. Snow White, if attired in an ordinary dress, cost $22; if the dress was made of silk, the doll cost as much as $36. Each dwarf doll cost $18, and the set included a number of forest animals. Snow White dolls were also manufactured by Knickerbocker Toys, which even offered a travelling case that would hold the entire miniature cast of the film's characters.

Many Snow White figurines have been produced over the years, some of the earliest of which were created by Brayton's Laguna Pottery. Snow White was also sold alongside Donald Duck and Pluto in a pack aptly named "Disney Fun Pals". But perhaps the most impressive – and expensive – of the porcelain items were the Capodimonte figures produced in 1984 by Italian sculptor Enzo Arzenton in a limited edition of 2,500 and priced between $1,590 and $1,850.

WALT DISNEY'S
Snow White and the Seven Dwarfs
EXCLUSIVE RECORDINGS
FROM THE ACTUAL SOUND FILM ON
"HIS MASTER'S VOICE"

PORTFOLIO No.1

The sleeve of a three-record set issued in Britain by His Master's Voice at the time of Snow White's release. Featuring "Exclusive Recordings from the Actual Sound Film", this was the first ever soundtrack recording of a feature film.

learn that working with others can be a satisfying experience as dozens of delightful creatures help Snow White with her chores".

Grenada issued a set of *Snow White and the Seven Dwarfs* postage stamps in 1980, the nine individual designs, which were accompanied by a souvenir sheet, being based on colour stills from the film.

As with every Disney movie before and since *Snow White and the Seven Dwarfs* inspired literally hundreds of comics, magazines and books, ranging from the expensive *Sketchbook of Snow White and the Seven Dwarfs*, with its tipped-in colour plates, to the popular *Snow White* Golden Stamp Book, with its perforated adhesive stickers. There were also cut-out books, puzzle books and painting books; the *Snow White Jingle Book* and the *Snow White Magic Mirror Book* with a pair of Magic Spectacles to view a series of stereoscopic pictures; there were give-away books advertising the American Dairy Association, Cheerios and Bendix Washing Machines, and a *Snow White and the Seven Dwarfs Recipe Book* issued by Armour ("Famous Flavour") Corned Beef.

Of the endless editions of the story itself, many contained alterations and embellishments

One reason for the popular success of *Snow White and the Seven Dwarfs* was its score of delightful songs, and these were soon available as sheet music and on a set of 78rpm records, which made history by being the first soundtrack recording of a feature film. Among the other records produced over the years have been a number of versions of the film and original stories featuring the dwarfs. Two of the songs originally planned for the film – "Music in Your Soup" and "You're Never Too Old to be Young" – were included on the album *The Seven Dwarfs and Their Diamond Mine*, and the dwarfs' "yodel" song was released on an album that introduced a new dance called "Doin' the Dopey".

In 1974 Disneyland Records presented an adaptation of Charles Dickens' *A Christmas Carol* with lyrics by Tom and Francis Adair and music by Buddy Baker. In this version the Spirit of Christmas Yet to Come turns out to be the Witch from *Snow White*.

A number of 8mm home movies were released in the late 1960s featuring highlights from Disney films including "Whistle While You Work" and "The Dwarfs' Dilemma" from *Snow White*, while the Walt Disney Educational Media Company launched *Snow White: A Lesson in Cooperation* for schools so that youngsters could

FATHER. MOTHER BABY

This painting of the Queen ordering Snow White's death is one of a series of colour plates included in *Walt Disney's Sketchbook of Snow White and the Seven Dwarfs*, produced in 1938 by the British publisher William Collins. The book also contained numerous sketches of the characters and settings in the film, such as those shown opposite.

Opposite: Snow White and her friends appeared on the covers of many periodicals such as this May 1938 issue of *Hollywood*, which ran a competition to find its readers' "favorite king of dwarfs". With the exception of Dopey, the dwarfs in this illustration are drawn in the style of the early inspirational sketches for the film, and are shown as having four fingers and a thumb.

Numerous activity books were produced to tie-in with *Snow White*, including *(right)* the *Golden Stamp Book* published in America and Britain in 1957, with 48 perforated pictures that could be gummed-in to illustrate the story; and *(below)* colouring books such as this one produced in Britain by William Collins.

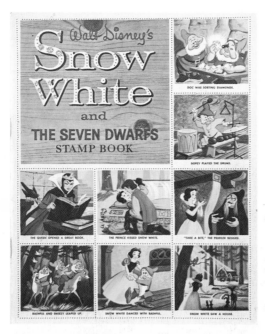

to what had appeared on the screen; and, on some occasions, used material from the early planning stages of the film.

At the very first studio conference on *Snow White*, Walt had described the film as opening with descriptive titles that would explain "how Snow White's Mother had died, and how the Queen had married the King, and how jealous the Queen was of Snow White".

Although the film never mentioned Snow White's mother, most of the earliest book versions – there were at least a dozen issued in America and Britain within the first year of the film's release – began with Snow White's mother wishing, as she does in the Grimm version, for a daughter "with lips as red as blood, skin as white as snow, and hair as black as the ebony of my embroidery frame". And illustrations showed the first Queen sitting by a window working at her embroidery, while a snow-storm raged outside.

Another early version of the story appeared in a colour newspaper strip syndicated in the

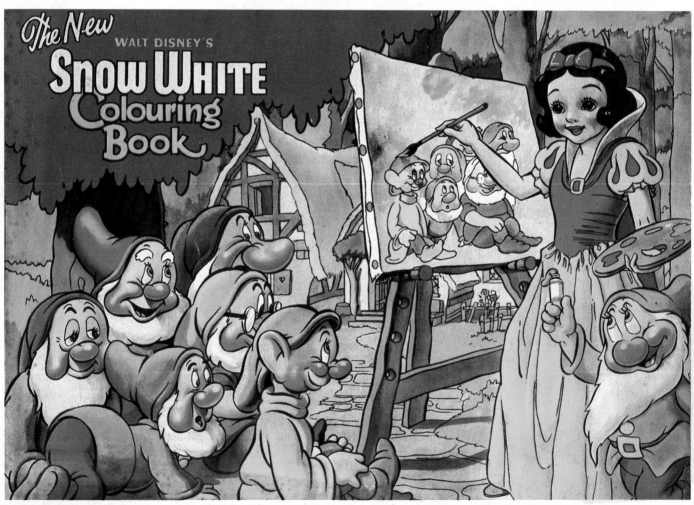

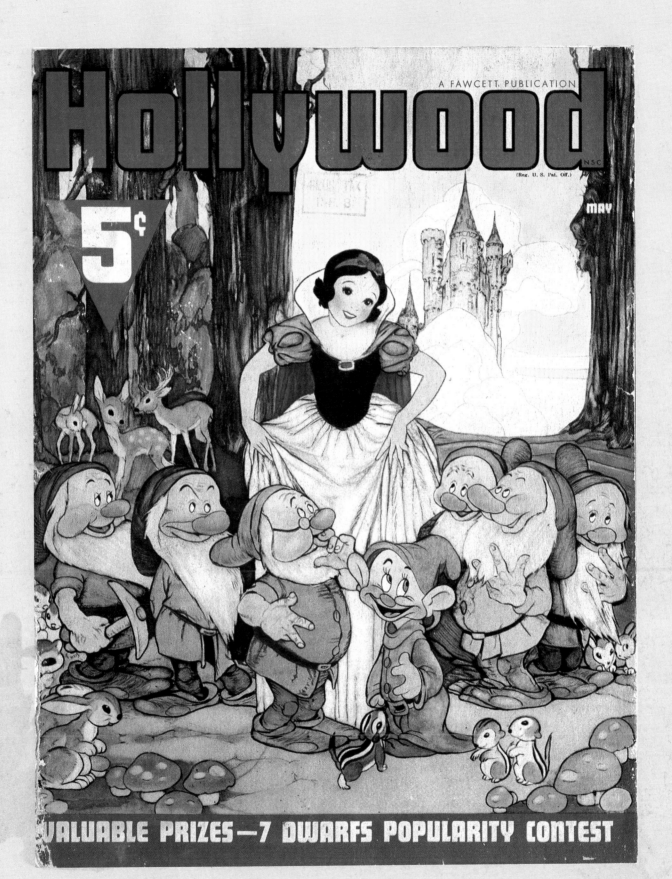

Dozens of different editions of the book-of-the-film were produced during the years immediately following the release of *Snow White*, including this one published in Britain by William Collins.

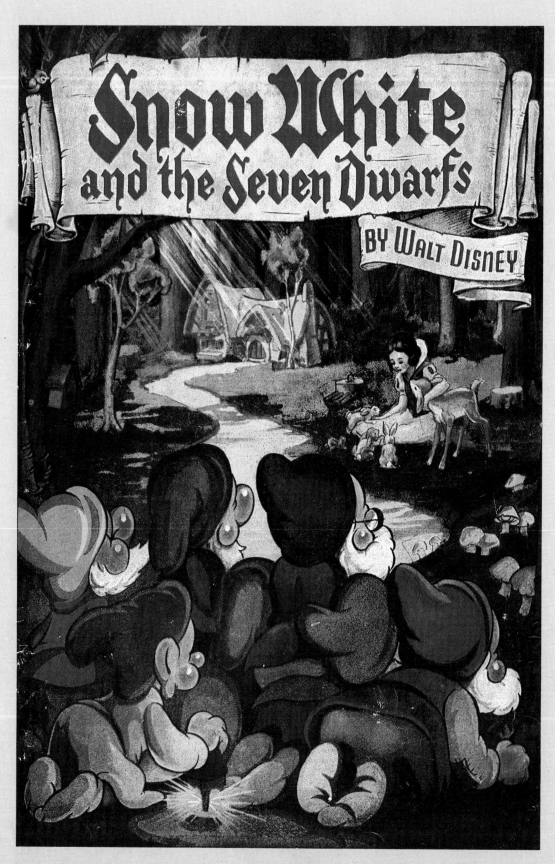

Although Snow White's real mother was never depicted in the film, she is referred to in numerous Disney story-books based on the movie. This is from the first story-book version published by Harper in 1937.

American Sunday papers, beginning in December 1937. Written by Merrill de Maris, who had worked on the screenplay, the story featured the Prince more prominently. Working in the castle-yard, Snow White dreams of the Prince who will one day rescue her from drudgery. "Do you want to see what my Prince will look like?" she asks a little blue-bird, and placing an up-turned wooden bucket on a post, she paints a face on it: "There he is! My Prince! Prince Buckethead!"

When the real Prince arrives, Snow White's wicked stepmother, here named Queen Grimhilde, has the young man locked up in the dungeons. "Fear not, my Princess!" he calls, as he is led away by the Queen's guards, "No power on earth can keep us apart!"

This was a return to the original scenario for the film and the Queen, now transformed into the Witch, accordingly pays the Prince a visit on her way to take the poisoned apple to Snow White. "You miserable hag!" cries the Prince, when he hears what she intends to do, "Such a vile plot can never succeed!" Eventually, the Prince manages to escape and "mounting his faithful horse ... speeds for the forest!" Like the dwarfs, he is too late to save Snow White – in fact, it takes him ages to find her, although when

he does, he soon awakens her with a kiss.

This beautifully rendered strip version (reprinted many times over the years) has appeared in publications throughout the world, including the French magazine *Le Journal de Mickey* and the British comic *Mickey Mouse Weekly*, which also contained colourful cut-outs of the characters and the words of the songs.

Some published versions contained additional lyrics to those used in the film. In several, for example, the Prince serenades Snow White with these words:

I've been searching everywhere
To find myself a lady fair,
Tra-la-la-la-la-la!
I'll not look any farther,
I'll win your heart and hand,
Because for me, you are,
The Fairest in the Land.

These books contain many interesting sidelights on the story not found in the film. When, for example, the Queen discovered that the box brought to her by the Huntsman contained "the heart of a beast" instead of that of Snow White, she "grew livid with anger and raising her arm, hurled the box at the mirror, shattering it in a thousand pieces. A little laugh

broke from each splinter of glass and grew and grew until her ears were filled with mocking laughter."

Included in several editions was the sequence, cut from the film, in which the dwarfs build a bed for Snow White: "Happy, using a tree for his tailoring shop, stitched away on the quilt. Spools of thread stood on little twigs like spindles, and a skein of bright wool was stretched between the antlers of a deer. Little birds flew back and forth unwinding the wool, while others snipped off lengths with their scissor-like beaks."

So many variations have been worked on the plot, that almost every book bearing the title *Walt Disney's Snow White and the Seven Dwarfs*, tells the story a little differently: in some, Snow White is not made to work as a scullery maid and is cast out only because the Queen is jealous of her beauty; other versions, following the original fairy-tale, introduce the Prince only at the end – just in time to revive Snow White.

In one book, the dwarfs are not only excused washing, they are actually allowed to help Snow White cook supper; and in another, more recent edition, none of the dwarfs are given names, except Doc. In the same book, the Witch is not killed but chased off into the forest by the animals, never to be seen again; while another re-telling has her fall to her death from the cliff,

not as a result of a lightning-bolt but because she wasn't looking where she was going.

Although there is no doubt about the finality of the Witch's fate in the film, she was obviously too good a character to be permanently laid to rest. The Dell comic *Disneyland Birthday Party*, published in 1958, revealed that the Witch had miraculously recovered from her fall into the ravine, and was up to her old tricks again. In this new adventure, the dwarfs find a huge diamond that grants wishes. They take it home and give it to Snow White; but, unbeknown to them, the Witch is lurking nearby and decides to steal the diamond for herself. She reduces her size and sneaks into the dwarfs' cottage to force Snow White to give up the diamond. Much to the Witch's horror, however, the diamond can only grant good wishes.

Once she was alive and kicking again, the Witch just couldn't be stopped: in the comic story "The Diamond Dust Dilemma" (1977), she turns the Princess to stone and, as the Prince is presumably wandering around the forest, it is the dwarfs who have to come to her rescue.

Books and comics have contained numerous extensions to the story. "Treasure Smile-Island" published in *Mickey Mouse Weekly* as early as 1938, told, for example, of an adventure that befell the dwarfs long before they met Snow

Opposite: The seven dwarfs have been featured in a variety of new adventures written and drawn for annuals and comics. This story appeared in the British publication *Mickey Mouse Weekly* on November 24, 1951.

White. And almost fifty years later, stories tell how Snow White goes back to visit the dwarfs after her marriage to the Prince, or how the dwarfs, trying to find a present for the third wedding anniversary of Snow White and her husband, stumble across the Magic Mirror.

One of the most curious of Snow White's new adventures is to be found in a role-playing book, *Snow White and the Enchanted Forest*, which requires the reader, representing the hero of the story, to make a series of correct decisions in order to rescue the Princess from several close encounters with the evil Queen.

As soon as the characters in *Snow White and*

the Seven Dwarfs were established as being part of the Disney family, they found themselves having adventures with characters from other movies. The dwarfs teamed up with Goofy and with Thumper the rabbit, and the Witch got involved in all kinds of things. In the comics, she vied with Captain Hook, the Big Bad Wolf and Mickey Mouse's arch-rival Black Pete, to become President of the "Bad Deeds Club", and, a few years later, rather surprisingly found herself helping Donald Duck's cousin Gladstone Gander give Christmas treats to a boys' home and admitting that she quite enjoyed the "good deed stuff" – even if it was only once a year!

Dopey wears a guilty expression as he steals a slice of Snow White's Christmas cake. This particular piece of artwork, specially drawn by the Disney artists, was accompanied by a poem and featured in the *Mickey Mouse Weekly* Christmas Special in 1939.

The comics provided artists and writers with any number of odd opportunities to feature Snow White and her friends. Among those found in the pages of *Mickey Mouse Weekly* were "Snow White's Party Page", which gave the rules for a variety of games, including (surprise, surprise) "The Wicked Witch", and "Dopey's Dictionary", which gave such humorous definitions as "Days: Patches of light punctuated by darkness. They are of different lengths . . . school days being very much longer than holi-days. And these have nothing to do with the kind of daze in which Goofy goes about."

In 1938, *Mickey Mouse Weekly* also produced the "Disneydrome": a model theatre offered free to readers (unless you lived overseas, when you were obliged to pay the princely sum of sixpence). "The 'Disneydrome'," announced the comic, "has been specially designed so that you can show the delightful stage version of Walt Disney's *Snow White and the Seven Dwarfs*, the 'actual speaking parts' for which are to be given exclusively in *Mickey Mouse Weekly* from now on."

The year after saw a stage version of the film for the *real* theatre. Presented by Jack Hylton at London's Victoria Palace, it featured players in grotesque masks based on the cartoon characters. Later, amateur thespians were able to try their hand when, in 1947, Silvey A. Clarke's six-act dramatization of the movie was published. The following year, the dwarfs donned skates to appear in *Ice Capades*, and they have since starred in any number of musicals, pantomimes and ice-shows.

A particularly curious adaptation of the story appeared on radio as a "Fractured Fairy-Tale" devised by the ventriloquist Edgar Bergen for The Lady Esther Screen Guild Theatre. Bergen was a friend of Walt Disney and was allowed a good deal of licence in re-telling the story with his dummies Mortimer Snerd and Charlie McCarthy, who had already met the dwarfs in the storybook, *Edgar Bergen's Charlie McCarthy Meets Walt Disney's Snow White*.

The radio show, sponsored by Lady Esther Cosmetics, was aired in December 1946, with Bergen providing the voice for Bashful: "I'm so bashful, I won't get undressed at night if *I'm* in the room!" Asked by Snow White how old he was, Bashful replied: "Oh, I don't know, it keeps changing every year!"

Bergen and his wooden companions cemented their relationship with Walt the following year, by starring in the film *Fun and Fancy Free*. Then, in December 1950, they made a zany appearance in Walt Disney's very first television programme,

One Hour in Wonderland, which was sponsored by Coca Cola and featured the Magic Mirror from *Snow White and the Seven Dwarfs*.

"It all started a good many years ago," explained Walt, "when I was travelling through Europe. I happened to meet a fairy princess who had a cousin who used to work here at the studio. She put me onto this wonderful Magic Mirror and I was finally able to buy it and I brought it back here to the studio."

Walt then spoke the words of the spell: "O, Slave in the Magic Mirror, come from the farthest space . . ."

"How hammy can you get!" muttered Charlie McCarthy.

The Slave appeared – portrayed by Hans Conried (later the voice of Captain Hook in Disney's *Peter Pan*) – and conjured up a series of film clips from *Snow White and the Seven Dwarfs* and other Disney films. When the Mirror got thirsty halfway through the show, he took a commercial break – and a reviving glass of Coca Cola!

The show was a huge success. "*One Hour in Wonderland*," announced the company's Annual Report, "has been hailed as an entertainment and production triumph throughout the nation. The show was greeted with a peak audience. With 10,500,000 television sets in operation, the Disney hour may have established a new viewing record." *Daily Variety* also praised the show and Hans Conried's performance as the "eerie slave of the Magic Mirror". Some years

Visitors to Disneyland in California, U.S.A., often have the pleasure of meeting Snow White and the Seven Dwarfs in person.

One of the ever-popular
Fantasyland attractions at
Disneyland is a "dark ride" based
on Snow White's adventures.
Shown (*right*) is an early concept
for the vehicle in which visitors
take their ride, and (*below*) a plan
of the complex layout for the
attraction, produced by the Disney
company's design subsidiary WED
(for Walter Elias Disney)
Enterprises Inc.

later, in 1958, the Mirror re-appeared in another
Disney television special, *Magic and Music*, this
time introducing sequences from *Melody Time*
and *Fantasia*.

In the meantime, the dwarfs had made their
own television debut at the opening of
Disneyland in 1955. And thirty years on, Snow
White and her seven little men can still be seen
at Disney's magical theme-park in California.
They take part in the daily parade (joined by the
Witch at Halloween), pose for photographs by
the Snow White Grotto and Wishing Well, and
mix with visitors lining up for admission to a
sinister gothic building where they can
experience "Snow White's Scary Adventures".

Inside, aboard a miniature mine-cart, you
travel through a three-dimensional visualization
of the film: passing through the dwarfs' cottage
and the diamond mine, you find yourself in the
Queen's dungeons where her infernal majesty is
busy at the cauldron and the skeletal remains of
former prisoners hang in chains from the wall.
Then you are running scared through the spooky
forest where bats fly up, twisted trees reach out
and grab at you with their branches, and the
Witch seems to lurk behind every rock and

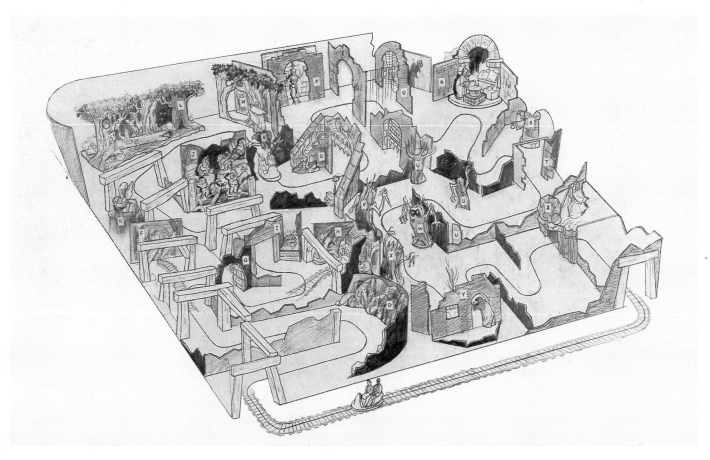

tree-stump with a poisoned apple in her hand. And, supposing you escape these terrors, then you still have to survive the Witch's final attempt on your life as she hurls a diamond the size of a boulder at your passing cart.

Similar attractions are to be found in Tokyo Disneyland and in the Magic Kingdom at Walt Disney World in Florida, which inspired one of the craziest of all the variations on the *Snow White* story. It appeared in a 1973 issue of the comic *Goofy and Pluto*, and it told how Goofy together with Pluto, Minnie Mouse and Jiminy Cricket set off on the Snow White ride at Walt

Disney World, only to find themselves in a strange country where they meet characters from *Alice in Wonderland* and then have to rescue the dwarfs who have been put under an evil spell by the perennially wicked Witch.

As for the film itself, it has lost none of its appeal. In January 1986, *Variety* listed *Snow White and the Seven Dwarfs* as 58th on its list of American and Canadian "All Time Film Rental Champs", with a figure of $41,400,000; and the world wide box-office revenue to date, is in excess of $83 million. And so they really have . . . lived happily ever after!

You can't travel far in "Snow White's Scary Adventures" at Disneyland, without encountering for yourself the cackling Witch whose evil schemes threatened Snow White's life.

Acknowledgements

The authors are greatly indebted to those people who generously reminisced about the *Snow White* era: Adriana Caselotti, Bill Cottrell, Jack Cutting, Roy E. Disney, Joe Grant, Ward Kimball, Diane Disney Miller and the late Wolfgang Reitherman; also to Robin Allan and Muir Hewitt who so willingly shared their expert knowledge.

Grateful thanks are also due to The Walt Disney Company, especially David R. Smith and Paula Sigman, for their advice and help with the text, and David Cleghorn and Brett Mattinson, for their hard work in unearthing and supplying illustrations. The cooperation and assistance of Greg Crosby is, as always, gratefully acknowledged.

Walt Disney
presents
SNOW WHITE AND THE SEVEN DWARFS
Adapted from
Grimm's Fairy Tales

Supervising Director
David Hand

Sequence Directors
Perce Pearce
Larry Morey
William Cottrell
Wilfred Jackson
Ben Sharpsteen

Supervising Animators
Hamilton Luske
Vladimir Tytla
Fred Moore
Norman Ferguson

Story Adaptation
Ted Sears
Otto Englander
Earl Hurd
Dorothy Ann Blank
Richard Creedon
Dick Rickard
Merrill De Maris
Webb Smith

Animators
Frank Thomas
Dick Lundy
Arthur Babbitt
Eric Larson
Milton Kahl
Robert Stokes
James Algar
Al Eugster
Cy Young
Joshua Meador
Ugo D'Orsi
George Rowley
Les Clark
Fred Spencer
Bill Roberts
Bernard Garbutt
Grim Natwick
Jack Campbell
Marvin Woodward
James Culhane
Stan Quackenbush
Ward Kimball
Wolfgang Reitherman
Robert Martsch

Character Designers
Albert Hurter
Joe Grant

Art Directors
Charles Philippi
Hugh Hennesy
Terrell Stapp
McLaren Stewart
Harold Miles
Tom Codrick
Gustaf Tenggren
Kenneth Anderson
Kendall O'Connor
Hazel Sewell

Backgrounds
Samuel Armstrong
Mique Nelson
Merle Cox
Claude Coats
Phil Dike
Ray Lockrem
Maurice Noble

Songs
Frank Churchill
Larry Morey

Music
Frank Churchill
Leigh Harline
Paul J Smith

Voice Talents
Adriana Caselotti .... Snow White
Harry Stockwell .... Prince Charming
Lucille La Verne .... The Queen
Moroni Olsen .... The Magic Mirror
Billy Gilbert .... Sneezy
Pinto Colvig .... Sleepy and Grumpy
Otis Harlan .... Happy
Scotty Mattraw .... Bashful
Roy Atwell .... Doc
Stuart Buchanan .... The Huntsman

Bibliography

Behlmer, Rudy, "They Called it 'Disney's Folly'" in *America's Favorite Movies: Behind the Scenes*, Frederick Ungar, New York, 1982

Charlot, Jean, *Art from the Mayans to Disney*, Sheed & Ward, London and New York, 1939

Culhane, Shamus, *Talking Animals and Other People*, St Martin's Press, New York, 1986

Feild, Robert D., *The Art of Walt Disney*, Collins, London and Glasgow; Macmillan, New York, 1942

Finch, Christopher, *The Art of Walt Disney: From Mickey Mouse to the Magic Kingdoms*, Harry N. Abrams, Inc., New York 1973

Finch, Christopher, *Walt Disney's America*, Abbeville Press Inc., New York, 1978

Grimm, Jacob and Wilhelm, *German Popular Stories* (translated from *Kinder und Haus Märchen* by Edgar Taylor), C. Baldwyn, London, 1823

Hulett, Steve, "The Making of Snow White and the Seven Dwarfs" in *Walt Disney's Snow White and the Seven Dwarfs*, Circle Fine Art Press, New York, 1978

Maltin, Leonard, *The Disney Films*, Crown Publishers, Inc., New York; Thomas Nelson, London, 1973 (revised edition 1984)

Miller, Diane Disney (as told to Pete Martin), *The Story of Walt Disney*, Henry Holt & Co., New York, 1957

Munsey, Cecil, *Disneyana: Walt Disney Collectibles*, Hawthorn Books, New York, 1974

Opie, Iona and Peter, *The Classic Fairy Tales*, Oxford University Press, London, 1974

Shale, Richard, *Donald Duck Joins Up: The Walt Disney Studio During World War II*, UMI Research Press, Ann Arbor, Michigan, 1982

Thomas, Bob, *Walt Disney: An American Original*, Simon & Schuster, New York, 1976 (published in London by New English Library as *The Walt Disney Biography*)

Tumbusch, Tom, *Tomart's Illustrated Disneyana Catalog and Price Guide* (3 volumes), Tomart Publications, Dayton, Ohio, 1975